ROUGH GUIDES **PHRASEBOOK**

SWEDISH

Contacting the Editors

Every effort has been made to provide accurate information in this publication, but changes are inevitable. The publisher cannot be responsible for any resulting loss, inconvenience or injury.
We would appreciate it if readers would call our attention to any errors or outdated information. We also welcome your suggestions; if you come across a relevant expression not in our phrase book, please contact us at:**hello@insightguides.com**

All Rights Reserved
© 2019 APA Publications (UK) Ltd.

Cover & Interior Design: Slawomir Krajewski
Head of Production: Rebeka Davies
Production Manager: Rebecca Hancock
Picture Researcher: Slawomir Krajewski
Cover Photo: all shutterstock

Interior Photos: all shutterstock

CONTENTS

INTRODUCTION

PRACTICALITIES

ON THE WAY

LEISURE TIME

SAFE TRAVEL

FOOD

PEOPLE

DICTIONARY

PRONUNCIATION

This section is designed to familiarize you with the sounds of Swedish using our simplified phonetic transcription. You'll find the pronunciation of the Swedish letters and sounds explained below, together with their 'imitated' equivalents. To use this system, found throughout the phrase book, simply read the pronunciation as if it were English, noting any special rules below.

The Swedish alphabet has 29 letters, the last three of which are the vowels å, ä and ö. Unlike English, the letter y is a vowel, meaning that Swedish has nine vowels. Swedish vowels are pure vowel sounds, as opposed to being a combination of two sounds (diphthongs) as they often are in English. Diphthongs occur only in dialects such as **Gotländska** (spoken on the island of Gotland), **Skånska** (spoken in the southern province of Skåne) and **Dalmål** (spoken in Dalarna, a province roughly in the middle of the country).

Swedish has very consistent rules with respect to the sounding of individual letters, i.e. all the letters should be pronounced distinctly, even vowels and consonants at the ends of words. The Swedish language is often referred to as a 'musical' language due to the fact that the intonation and rhythm moves up and down, giving the language a musical quality. Despite this stress, pronunciation is quite consistent. Most words with two or more syllables have primary stress on the first syllable of the word, and this can be followed by a secondary stress on the second syllable. There are also a number of words with two or more syllables which do not have stress on the first syllable, but often on the last. Stress has been noted in the phonetic transcription with underlining.

CONSONANTS

Letter	Approximate Pronunciation	Symbol	Example	Pronunciation
c	like s in sit	s	cykel	<u>sew</u> • kerl*
g	1. before o, å, a and u, like g in get	g	gata	<u>gah</u> • ta
	2. before i, e, ö and ä, like y in yet	y	get	y<u>et</u>
	3. after r and l, like y in yet	y	borg	bohry
j	1. soft, like y in yet	y	jag	yahg
	2. after r and l, like y in yet	y	familj	fah • <u>mihly</u>
k	1. before o, å, a and u, like k in keep	k	katt	kat
	2. before i, e, ö and ä, like ch in chew		köpa	<u>chur</u> • pa
q	like k in keep	k	Blomquist	<u>bloom</u> • kvihst
r	strong, almost trilled, r		röd	rurd
s	like s in see	s	sitta	<u>siht</u> • a
w	like v in very	v	wennergren	<u>vehn</u> • eh • gr<u>ehn</u>
z	like s in suit	s	zebra	<u>see</u> • bra

Letters b, d, f, h, m, n, p, t, v and x are pronounced as in English.
*Bold indicates a lengthening of the sound — emphasis on the vowel sound.

CONSONANT CLUSTERS

Letter	Approximate Pronunciation	Symbol	Example	Pronunciation
ch	like sh in ship	sh	check	_sheh_k
ck	like ck in tick	k	flicka	_flih_ • ka
dj, gj, hj, lj	like y in yet	y	djur	_yeur_
sj, skj, stj, sch, ch	like sh in shop	sh	sjal	_shahl_
sk	1. before o, å, a and u, like sk in skip	sk	skala	_skah_ • la
	2. before i, e, ö and ä, like sh in ship	sh	skära	_shai_ • ra
tj	like sh followed by ch	shch	tjock	_shchohk_

VOWELS

Letter	Approximate Pronunciation	Symbol	Example	Pronunciation
a	1. when long, like a in father	ah	dag	_dahg_
	2. when short, like a in cat	a	katt	_kat_
e	1. when long, like ee in beer	ee	veta	_vee_ • ta
	2. when short, like e in fell	eh	ett	_eht_

Letter	Approximate Pronunciation	Symbol	Example	Pronunciation
i	1. when long, like ee in see	ee	bil	*beel*
	2. when short, like i in bit	ih	mitt	*miht*
o	1. when long, like oa in coat	oa	sko	*skoa*
	2. like the exclamation oh	oh	font	*fohnt*
u	1. when long, eu in feud	eu	ruta	*reu • ta*
	2. when short, like u in up	uh	uppe	*uh • per*
y	like ew in new	ew	byta	*bew • ta*
å	1. when long, like oa in oar	oa	gå	*goa*
	2. when short, like o in hot	oh	åtta	*oh • ta*
ä	1. when long, like ai in air	ai	här	*hair*
	2. when short, like e in set	eh	säng	*sehng*
ö	1. when long, like u in cure	ur	smör	*smur*
	2. when short, like u in nut	uh	rött	*ruhrt*

Swedish vowels are divided into two groups: hard and soft. **A, o, u** and **å** are hard vowels; **e, i, y, ä** and **ö** are soft vowels. Vowels can also be pronounced either long or short. When a vowel is pronounced 'long' the sound is longer, but also more open and rounder. The 'short' vowel sounds are more closed, literally a 'shorter' sound than a long vowel. An easy rule to remember is that if the vowel is followed by a single consonant, as in **stad** (city), it is long. If the vowel is followed by a double consonant, as in **katt** (cat), the vowel is short. The exception to this rule is with the consonants **m** and **n**.

Swedish is spoken throughout Sweden as well as in the coastal regions of Finland and Estonia. While written Swedish has been standardized, there are characteristic spoken dialects in certain regions such as Gotland, Skåne and Dalarna. Other languages, in addition to Swedish, are also spoken in Sweden, such as Finnish, which is spoken in some communities in Northern Sweden, and the Sámi (Lappish) languages, which are spoken in Sámi communities throughout Northern Norway, Sweden, Finland and Russia. Swedish, Norwegian, Danish, Icelandic and Faroese (spoken on the Faroe Islands) are all derived from Old Norse, the language spoken prior to the Viking Age. Over time, the Scandinavian languages developed from this common language. Danish, Norwegian and Swedish are separate and distinct languages but remain close enough that they are mutually intelligible. The Finnish and Sámi languages belong to a different language family, to which Hungarian also belongs.

HOW TO USE THE APP

Quickly access your recently viewed entries

Look up words and phrases on-the-go

Conveniently navigate the phrasebook categories

Change font size and background color

Save the most useful everyday words and phrases to your Favorites

Use the Flash Cards Quiz to learn and memorize new words easily

Spanish Phrasebook

Can you recommend a good restaurant/ bar?
¿Puede recomend... ...n buen
restaurante/bar?
pweh•deh reh•koh•_mehn_•_dahr_•meh
oon bwehn rehs•taw•_rahn_•teh/bahr

Take all digital advantages of the app: listen to words and phrases pronounced by native speakers

Is there a t...

Phrasebook   Tools   Catalogue   Favourites   Info

To learn how to Activate the app, see the inside back cover of this phrasebook.

GRAMMAR

REGULAR VERBS

The present tense of regular verbs in Swedish is formed by adding either -**r** or -**er** to the stem. If the stem ends in **a**, add an -**r**, if it ends in a consonant add -**er**. The past tense is formed by adding either -**de** or -**te** to the basic form. If the basic form ends in a **p**, **t**, **k** or **s**, add -**te**, if not then add -**de**. The future is formed by adding the present tense of **ska** (will) + the verb in the infinitive. This applies to all persons (e.g., I, you, he, she, it, etc.). Following are the present, past and future forms of the verbs **att köpa** (to buy) and **att fråga** (to ask). The different conjugation endings are in bold.

	PRESENT	PAST	FUTURE
att köpa (to buy)	köpe**r**	köp**te**	*ska köpa*
att fråga (to ask)	fråga**r**	fråga**de**	*ska fråga*

PRONOUNS

I	jag	it (common/neuter)	den/det
you (sing., inf.)	du	we	vi
he	han	you (pl.)	ni
she	hon	they	de

In Swedish there are two terms for 'you': **du** (singular/informal) and **ni** (plural/informal). Both are used when talking to relatives, friends, colleagues, children, between young people and in work situations. The plural form, **ni**, is used in more formal situations to refer to one or more persons. Its use has however become less frequent, so nowadays you will hear most people address each other with **du**.

IRREGULAR VERBS

There are a number of irregular verbs in Swedish; these must be memorized. Like regular verbs, however, the irregular verb form remains the same, irrespective of person. The table below shows the present, past and future conjugations for a number of important, useful irregular verbs.

	PRESENT	PAST	FUTURE
att vara (to be)	**är**	**var**	*ska vara*
att ha (to have)	**har**	**hade**	*ska ha*
att komma (to come) *komma*	**kommer**	**kom**	*ska*
att göra (to do)	**gör**	**gjorde**	*ska göra*
att gå (to go/walk)	**går**	**gick**	*ska gå*

sing. = singular, inf. = informal, pl. = plural

WORD ORDER

Swedish is similar to English in terms of word order for simple
sentences, i.e. it follows the subject-verb-object pattern.
Example:
Sara läser en bok. Sara is reading a book.
When the sentence doesn't begin with a subject, the word
order changes; the verb and the subject are inverted.
Example:
Nu läser Sara en bok. Now Sara is reading a book.
However, **nu** could just as well be placed at the end of the
sentence, e.g. **Sara läser en bok nu.**
Questions are formed by reversing the order of the subject and
verb:
Du ser katten. You see the cat.
Ser du katten? Do you see the cat?

NEGATIONS

A statement can be negated by inserting the word **inte** after
the verb:
Jag talar svenska. I speak Swedish.
Jag talar inte svenska. I do not speak Swedish.

NOUNS & ARTICLES

The indefinite article (a, an) is expressed with **en** for common nouns and with **ett** for neuter nouns. Generally, common nouns can be both feminine and masculine (e.g. people, animals, etc.); neuter nouns have no gender (e.g. house, roof, etc.). However, there are several exceptions to this rule.

In Swedish, there are five different endings used to form plural nouns; three correspond to common gender nouns and two to neuter gender nouns. The following rules apply to nouns in the indefinite singular.

1. **en** words that end in -**a** take an -**or** ending
2. **en** words that end in -**e** take an -**ar** ending
3. **en** words with stress on the last vowel take an -**er** ending
4. **ett** words that end in a vowel take an -**n** ending
5. **ett** words that end in a consonant take no additional ending

Common gender nouns that end in a consonant are not covered by the rules above. These words will take either an -**ar** ending or an -**er** ending. The nouns which fall into this category will simply need to be memorized.

SINGULAR INDEFINITE	PLURAL INDEFINITE
en flicka (a girl)	flick*or*
en timme (an hour)	timm*ar*
en telefon (a telephone)	telefon*er*
ett konto (an account)	kont*on*
ett hus (a house)	hus
en bil (a car)	bil*ar*

Definite articles: where in English we say 'the car', the Swedes say the equivalent of 'car-the', i.e. they tag the definite article onto the end of the noun. In the singular, common nouns take an -**en** ending, neuter nouns an -**et** ending. In the plural, common nouns add an -**na** and neuter nouns take an -**en** ending, neuter nouns an -**et** ending. In the plural, common nouns add an -**na** and neuter nouns take an -**en**.

	SINGULAR	PLURAL
common gender	katten the cat	katterna the cats
neuter gender	tårget the train	tågen the trains

DEMONSTRATIVE ADJECTIVES

	SINGULAR	NEUTER	PLURAL
this/these	min	mitt	mina
these/those	den	det	de
	denna bil (this car)	deta hus (this house)	

POSSESSIVE ADJECTIVES

	COMMON	NEUTER	PLURAL
my	min	mitt	mina
your (sing.)	din	ditt	dina
our	vår	vårt	våra
his	hans	ditt	dina
hers		hennes	
its		dess/dess	
their		deras	
your (pl.)	er	ert	era

ADVERBS & ADVERBIAL EXPRESSIONS

Adverbs are generally formed by adding -t to the corresponding adjective.
Snabb quick
Hon går snabbt. She walks quickly.

PRACTICALITIES

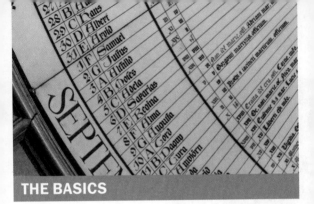

THE BASICS

NUMBERS

NEED TO KNOW

0	**noll**	*nohl*
1	**ett**	*eht*
2	**två**	*tvoa*
3	**tre**	*tree*
4	**fyra**	*<u>few</u> • ra*
5	**fem**	*fehm*
6	**sex**	*sehx*
7	**sju**	*sheu*
8	**åtta**	*oh • <u>ta</u>*
9	**nio**	*<u>nee</u> • oa*
10	**tio**	*<u>tee</u> • oa*
11	**elva**	*<u>ehl</u> • va*
12	**tolv**	*tohlv*
13	**tretton**	*<u>treh</u> • tohn*
14	**fjorton**	*<u>fyeur</u> • tohn*
15	**femton**	*<u>fehm</u> • tohn*

16	**sexton** _sehx_ • _tohn_
17	**sjutton** _sheu_ • _tohn_
18	**arton** _ar_ • _tohn_
19	**nitton** _nih_ • _tohn_
20	**tjugo** _shcheu_ • _goa_
21	**tjugoett** _shcheu_ • _goa_ • _eht_
22	**tjugotvå** _shcheu_ • _goa_ • _tvoa_
30	**trettio** _treh_ • _tee_ • _oa_
31	**trettioett** _treh_ • _tee_ • _oa_ • _eht_
40	**fyrtio** _fuhr_ • _tee_ • _oa_
50	**femtio** _fehm_ • _tee_ • _oa_
60	**sextio** _sehx_ • _tee_ • _oa_
70	**sjuttio** _sheu_ • _tee_ • _oa_
80	**åttio** _oh_ • _tee_ • _oa_
90	**nittio** _nih_ • _tee_ • _oa_
100	**hundra** _huhn_ • _dra_
101	**hundraett** _huhn_ • _dra_ • _eht_
200	**två hundra** _tvoa_ _huhn_ • _dra_
500	**fem hundra** _fehm_ _huhn_ • _dra_
1,000	**ett tusen** _eht_ _teu_ • _sehn_
10,000	**tio tusen** _tee_ • _oa_ _teu_ • _sehn_
1,000,000	**en miljon** _ehn_ _mihl_ • _yoan_

ORDINAL NUMBERS

first	**första**
	furs • _ta_
second	**andra**
	_an_ • _dra_
third	**tredje**
	tree • _dyer_

fourth	**fjärde** *fyair • der*
fifth	**femte** *fehm • ter*
once	**en gång** *ehn goang*
twice	**två gånger** *tvoa goang • ehr*
three times	**tre gånger** *tree goang • ehr*

TIME

NEED TO KNOW

What time is it?	**Hur mycket är klockan?** *heur mew • ker air kloh • kan*
It's noon [midday].	**Klockan är tolv.** *kloh • kan air tolv*
Midnight.	**Midnatt.** *meed • nat*
From 9 o'clock to 5 o'clock.	**Från nio till sjutton.** *froan nee • oa tihl sheu • tohn*
It's twenty after [past] four.	**Den är tjugo över fyra.** *dehn air shcheu • goa ur • ver few • ra*
It's a quarter to nine.	**Den är kvart i nio.** *dehn air kvart ee nee • oa*
5:30 a.m.	**Halv sex på morgonen.** *halv sehx poa mor • oh • nehn*
5:30 p.m.	**Halv sex på kvällen.** *halv sehx poa kveh • lehn*

Sweden officially follows the 24-hour clock. Formal communication, such as public transporation schedules and TV programming, follows this system. However, in ordinary conversation, time is generally expressed as shown above, often with the addition of **på morgonen** (in the morning), **på förmiddagen** (mid-morning), **på eftermiddagen** (in the afternoon), **på kvällen** (in the evening) and **på natten** (at night).

DAYS

NEED TO KNOW

Monday	**måndag**
	moan • _dahg_
Tuesday	**tisdag**
	tees • _dahg_
Wednesday	**onsdag**
	oans • _dahg_
Thursday	**torsdag**
	toash • _dahg_
Friday	**fredag**
	free • _dahg_
Saturday	**lördag**
	lurr • _dahg_
Sunday	**söndag**
	surn • _dahg_

DATES

yesterday	**igår**
	ee • goar
today	**idag**
	ee • dahg
tomorrow	**imorgon**
	ee • mo • ron
day	**dag**
	dahg
week	**vecka**
	veh • ka
month	**månad**
	moa • nad
year	**år**
	oar

MONTHS

January	**januari**
	ya • neu • ah • ree
February	**februari**
	fehb • reu • ah • ree
March	**mars**
	mash
April	**april**
	ap • rihl
May	**maj**
	maiy
June	**juni**
	yeu • nee
July	**juli**
	yeu • lee

August	**augusti**	
	a • <u>guhss</u> • tee	
September	**september**	
	sehp • <u>tehm</u> • behr	
October	**oktober**	
	ohk • <u>toa</u> • behr	
November	**november**	
	noh • <u>vehm</u> • behr	
December	**december**	
	dee • <u>sehm</u> • behr	

Sweden follows a day-month-year format instead of the month-day-year format used in the U.S.
E.g.: July 25, 2008; **25/07/08** = 7/25/2008 in the U.S.

SEASONS

spring	**vår**
	voar
summer	**sommar**
	<u>soh</u> • mar
fall [autumn]	**höst**
	huhst
winter	**vinter**
	<u>vihn</u> • tehr

HOLIDAYS

January 1: **Nyårsdagen** New Year's Day
January 6: **Trettondagen** Epiphany
May 1: **Första maj** May Day
June 6: **Flaggans dag** Flag Day

December 25: **Juldagen** Christmas Day
December 26: **Annandag jul** Boxing Day
Moveable dates include:
Långfredagen Good Friday
Kristi himmelfärdsdag Ascension
Pingstdagen Whitsunday
Allhelgonadagen All Saints' Day
Midsommardagen Midsummer Day

The two most important holidays in Sweden are
Midsummer and Christmas. **Midsommardagen**
(Midsummer) is celebrated with midsummer poles (similar
to the may pole) and traditional songs and dances.
Traditional food includes **matjesill** (pickled herring), fresh
fish and schnapps. For **Juldagen** (Christmas), special
cakes and other delicious treats are prepared, such as
pepparkakor (ginger cookies), **saffranbullar** (saffron
buns) and **julbord** (Christmas **smörgåsbord,** a festive
buffet). Though not an official holiday, **Luciadagen**
(St. Lucia Day) on December 13 marks the beginning
of the Chirstmas season. Swedes also celebrate the
beginning of spring on April 30, which is known as
Valborgsmässoafton, with huge bonfires, fireworks and
singing. June 6 is **Flaggans dag** (Flag Day), the national
day of Sweden. Streets are decorated with yellow and blue,
the colors of the Swedish flag, patriotic speeches are made
and traditional games and meals are enjoyed.

ARRIVAL & DEPARTURE

NEED TO KNOW

I'm here on vacation [holiday]/business.	**Jag är här på semester/ affärsresa.**
	Yahg air hair poa seh • mehs • ter/ a • fairs • ree • sa
I'm going to…	**Jag ska resa till…**
	yahg skah ree • sa tihl…
I'm staying at a hotel/youth hostel.	**Jag bor på hotell/vandrarhem.**
	yahg boar poa hoh • tehl/ vahnd • rar • hehm

BORDER CONTROL

I'm just passing through.	**Jag är bara på genomresa.**
	yahg air bah • ra poa ye • nohm • ree • sa
I would like to declare…	**Jag skulle vilja förtulla…**
	yahg skuh • ler vihl • ya furr • tuh • la…
I have nothing to declare.	**Jag har inget att förtulla.**
	yahg hahr ihng • eht at furr • tuh • la

YOU MAY HEAR...

Er biljett/Ert pass, tack.
eer bihl•yeht/ eert pas tak

Your ticket/ passport, please.

Vad är syftet med ert besök?
vahd air sewf•tet meed ehrt beh•surk

What's the purpose of your visit?

Var bor du?
vahr boar deu

Where are you staying?

Hur länge ska du stanna?
heur lehng•er skah deu stan•a

How long are you staying?

Vem är du här med?
vehm air deu hair meed

Who are you here with?

Metta le iniziali/Firmi qui.
meht•tah leh ee•nee•tsyah•lee/ feer•mee kwee

Initial/Sign here.

YOU MAY SEE...

TULL
customs

TAXFRIA VAROR
duty-free goods

VAROR ATT FÖRTULLA
goods to declare

INGET ATT FÖRTULLA
nothing to declare

PASSKONTROLL
passport control

POLIS
police

YOU MAY HEAR...

Har du något att förtulla?
hahr deu noa • goht at furr • tuh • la

Anything to declare?

Du måste betala tull för det här.
deu mos • ter beh • tah • la tuhl furr dee hair

You must pay duty on this.

Var snäll och öppna den här väskan.
vahr snehl ohk urp • na dehn hair vehs • kan

Please open this bag.

MONEY

NEED TO KNOW

Where's...?	**Var ligger...?** *vahr lih • gehr...*
the ATM	**bankomaten** *bank • oa • mah • tehn*
the bank	**banken** *bank • ehn*
the currency exchange office	**växelkontoret** *vehx • ehl • kohn • toar • eht*
What time does the bank open/close?	**När öppnar/stänger banken?** *nair urp • nahr/stehng • ehr bank • ehn*
I'd like to change dollars/pounds into kronor.	**Jag skulle vilja växla dollar/pund till kronor.** *yahg skuh • ler vihl • ya vehx • la doh • lar/pund tihl kroa • nohr*
I want to cash some traveler's checks [cheques].	**Jag skulle vilja lösa in några resecheckar.** *yahg skuh • ler vihl • ya lur • sa ihn noa • gra ree • seh • sheh • kar*

AT THE BANK

Can I exchange foreign currency here?	**Kan jag växla pengar här?** *kan yahg <u>vehx</u> • la <u>pehng</u> • ar hair*
What's the exchange rate?	**Vad är växelkursen?** *vahd air <u>vehx</u> • ehl • keur • shehn*
I think there's a mistake.	**Jag tror det är ett misstag.** *Yahg troar dee air eht mis • tagh*
How much is the fee?	**Hur mycket är expeditionsavgiften?** *Heur <u>mew</u> • ker air ehx • peh • dee • <u>shoans</u> • afv • <u>yihf</u> • tehn*
I've lost my traveler's checks.	**Jag har tappat mina resecheckar.** *Yahg hahr <u>ta</u> • pat <u>mee</u> • na <u>ree</u> • seh • sheh • kar*
I've lost my card.	**Jag har tappat mitt kort.** *yahg hahr <u>ta</u> • pat miht koart*
My credit cards have been stolen.	**Mina kreditkort är stulna.** *<u>mee</u> • na kreh • <u>deet</u> • koart air <u>steul</u> • na*
My card doesn't work.	**Mitt kort fungerar inte.** *miht koart fuhn • <u>gee</u> • rar <u>ihn</u> • ter*
The ATM ate my card.	**Uttagsautomaten tog mitt kort.** *eut • tahgs • ah • toa • mah • tehn toagh mith koart.*

For Numbers, see page 22.

YOU MAY SEE...

SÄTT IN KORTET	insert card
AVBESTÄLLA	cancel
RENSA	clear
ENTER	enter
PINKOD	PIN
TA UT	withdraw
FRÅN CHEKKONTO	from checking [current] account
FRÅN SPARKONTO	from savings account
KVITTOT	receipt

Cash can be obtained from a **Bankomat** (ATM) with MasterCard, Visa, Eurocard, American Express and other international credit cards or with a debit card. It is also possible to exchange traveler's checks in Sweden. In recent years, it has become quite common for the banks to refer customers with traveler's checks to the nearest **växelkontor** (currency exchange business) such as Forex or X-Change. These businesses are often located near or in points of departure/arrival such as airports or train stations, but can also be found in city centers. Remember to bring your passport with you for identification when you want to exchange money or cash traveler's checks. Most banks close at 3:00 p.m., though some are open later one day a week, often on Thursdays.

YOU MAY SEE...

Unlike the majority of other European Union countries, Sweden has not adopted the euro as its national currency. Sweden's monetary unit is the **krona** (singular) or **kronor** (plural) abbreviated to **SEK**.
The **krona** is divided into **öre**.
Coins: 50 **öre**,1 **krona**, 5 and 10 **kronor**
Banknotes: 20, 50,100, 500 and 1000 **kronor**

CONVERSATION

NEED TO KNOW

Hello!	**Hej!**
	hay
How are you?	**Hur står det till?**
	heur stoar dee tihl
Fine, thanks.	**Bra, tack. Och du?**
And you?	*brah tak ohk deu*
Excuse me!	**Ursäkta!**
	eur • shehk • ta
Do you speak	**Talar du engelska?**
English?	*tah • lar deu ehng • ehl • ska*
What's your name?	**Vad heter du?**
	vahd hee • tehr deu
My name is...	**Jag heter...**
	yahg hee • tehr...

Nice to meet you.	**Trevligt att träffas.**
	treev • lihgt at trehf • as.
Where are you from?	**Var kommer du ifrån?**
	vahr ko • mehr deu ee • froan
I'm from the U.S./U.K.	**Jag kommer från USA/ Storbritannien.**
	yahg koh • mehr froan eu ehs ah/ stoap • bree • tan • yehn
What do you do?	**Vad sysslar du med?**
	vahd sews • lar deu meed
I work for…	**Jag jobbar på.**
	yahg yohb • ar poa…
I'm a student.	**Jag är student.**
	yahg air stuh • dent
I'm retired.	**Jag är pensionär.**
	yahg air pang • shoa • nair
Do you like…?	**Tycker du om…?**
	tew • kehr deu ohm…
Goodbye.	**Hej då.**
	hay • doa
See you later.	**Vi ses.**
	vee sees

LANGUAGE DIFFICULTIES

Do you speak English?	**Talar du engelska?** *tah • lar deu ehng • ehl • ska*
Does anyone here speak English?	**Talar någon engelska här?** *tah • lar noa • gohn ehng • ehl • ska hair*
I don't speak Swedish.	**Jag talar inte svenska.** *yahg tah • lar ihn • ter svehn • ska*
Could you speak more slowly?	**Kan du tala lite långsammare?** *kan deu tah • la lee • ter loang • sam • a • rer*
Could you repeat that?	**Kan du upprepa det?** *kan deu uhp • ree • pah dee*
Excuse me?	**Ursäkta?** *eur • shehk • ta*
What was that?	**Vad var det?** *vahd vahr dee*
Can you spell it?	**Kan du stava det?** *kahn deu stah • va deht*
Write it down, please.	**Skriv ner det, tack.** *skreev neer dee tak*
Can you translate this for me?	**Kan du översätta det här?** *kan deu ur • ver • seh • ta deet hair*
What does this/that mean?	**Vad betyder det här/där?** *vad beh • tew • der dee hair/dair*
I understand.	**Jag förstår.** *yahg furr • stoar*
I don't understand.	**Jag förstår inte.** *yahg furr • stoar ihn • ter*
Do you understand?	**Förstår du?** *furr • stoar deu*

YOU MAY HEAR...

Jag talar bara lite engelska.
*yahg tah • lar bah • ra lee • ter
ehng • ehl • ska*

I speak only
a little English.

Jag talar inte engelska.
yahg tah • lar in • ter ehng • ehl • ska

I don't speak
English.

MAKING FRIENDS

Swedes shake hands when greeting someone
and when saying goodbye; this applies for meeting new
people but is also often the case with colleagues or
acquaintances. When you meet someone for the first time,
shake hands and give your name. As in many countries,
titles are more commonly used by the older generation, but
you will sometimes hear **herr** (Mr.), **fru** (Mrs.) and **fröken**
(Miss) used, as well as professional titles, e.g., **doktor**
(doctor), **ingenjör** (engineer), etc.

Hello.	**Hej.**
	hay
Good morning.	**God morgon.**
	goad mor • on
Good afternoon.	**God middag.**
	goad mi • dahg
Good evening.	**God afton.**
	goad af • tohn
My name is...	**Jag heter...**
	yahg hee • tehr...
What's your name?	**Vad heter du?**
	vahd hee • tehr deu

I'd like to introduce you to...	**Får jag presentera...**
	foar yahg preh • sehn • tee • ra...
Pleased to meet you.	**Trevligt att träffas.**
	treev • lihgt at treh • fas
How are you?	**Hur står det till?**
	heur stoar dee tihl
Fine, thanks.	**Bra, tack.**
	brah tak
And you?	**Och du?**
	ohk deu

TRAVEL TALK

I'm here...	**Jag är här...**
	yahg air hair...
on business	**på affärsresa**
	poa a • fairs • ree • sa
on vacation [holiday]	**på semester**
	poa seh • mehs • tehr
studying	**för studier**
	furr steu • de • ehr
I'm staying for...	**Jag ska stanna i...**
	yahg skah sta • na ee...
I've been here..	**Jag har varit här i...**
	yahg hahr vah • riht hair ee...
a day	**en dag**
	ehn dahg
a week	**en vecka**
	ehn veh • ka
a month	**en månad**
	ehn moa • nad
Where are you from?	**Var kommer du ifrån?**
	vahr koh • mehr deu ee • froan
I'm from.	**Jag kommer från.**
	yahg koh • mehr froan...

For Numbers, see page 22.

PERSONAL

Who are you here with?	**Vem är du här med?**
	vehm air deu hair meed
I'm on my own.	**Jag är ensam.**
	yahg air ehn•sam
I'm with…	**Jag är här med…**
	yahg air hair meed…
my husband/wife	**min man/fru**
	mihn man/freu
my boyfriend	**min pojkvän**
	mihn povk•vehn
girlfriend	**flickvän**
	flihk•vehn
a friend/friends	**en vän/vänner**
	ehn vehn/venhn•ehr
a colleague	**en kollega**
	ehn koh•lee•ga/
colleagues	**kolleger**
	koh•lee•goahr
When's your birthday?	**När fyller du år?**
	nair fewl•ehr deu oar
How old are you?	**Hur gammal är du?**
	heur gah•mal air deu
I'm…	**Jag är…**
	yahg air…
single	**ogift**
	oa•yift
in a relationship	**i ett förhållande**
	ee eht furr•hoal•an•der
engaged	**förlovad**
	fuhr•loh•vad

married	**gift**
	yihft
divorced	**skild**
	shihld
separated	**separerad**
	seh • pa • ree • rad
I'm a widow/	**Jag är änka/änkling.**
widower.	*yahg air ehng • ka/ehnak • lihna*
Do you have children/	**Har du barn/barnbarn?**
grandchildren?	*hahr deu bahrn/bahrn • bahrn*

For Numbers, see page 22.

WORK & SCHOOL

What do you do?	**Vad sysslar du med?**
	vahd sews • lar deu meed
What are you	**Vad läser du?**
studying?	*vahd lai • sehr deu*
I'm studying…	**Jag läser…**
	yahg lai • sehr…
I work full time/	**Jag arbetar heltid/deltid.**
part time.	*yahg ahr • beh • tar hehl • teed/dehl • teed*
I work at home.	**Jag arbetar hemifrån.**
	yahg ahr • beh • tar hehm • ih • froan
I'm unemployed.	**Jag är arbetslös.**
	yahg air ar • behts • lus
Who do you work for?	**Vilken firma jobbar du på?**
	vihl • kehn fihr • ma yohb • ar deu poa
I work for…	**Jag jobbar på…**
	yahg yohb • ar poa…
Here's my business	**Här är mitt kort.**
card.	*hair air miht koahrt*

WEATHER

What's the weather forecast for tomorrow?	**Vad är väderleksrapporten för imorgon?** *vahd air vair • dehr • leeks • ra • pohr • tehn furr ee • mo • ron*
What beautiful/ terrible weather!	**Vilket vackert/förskräckligt väder!** *vihl • keht va • kert/furr • skrehk • ligt vair • dehr*
It's...	**Det är...** *dee air...*
hot/cold	**varmt/kallt** *varmt/kahlt*
cool/warm	**svalt/varmt** *svahlt/varmt*
rainy/sunny	**regnigt/soligt** *rehng • nihkt/soal • ikt*
snowy/icy	**snöigt/halt** *snur • ikt/hahlt*
Do I need a jacket/ an umbrella?	**Behöver jag en jacka/ett paraply?** *beh • hur • ver yahg ehn yah • ka/eht pa • ra • plew*

ON THE WAY

GETTING AROUND

NEED TO KNOW

How do I get to town?	**Hur kommer jag till staden?**
	heur <u>koh</u> • mehr yahg tihl <u>stahd</u> • ehn
Where is...?	**Var ligger...?**
	vahr <u>lih</u> • gehr...
the airport	**flygplatsen**
	<u>flewg</u> • plats • ehn
the train [railway] station	**järnvägsstationen**
	yairn • vehgs • sta • <u>shoa</u> • nehn
the bus station	**bussterminalen**
	bus • tehr • <u>mee</u> • nah • lehn
the subway [underground] station	**tunnelbanestationen**
	<u>teu</u> • nehl • bah • neh • sta • <u>shoan</u> • ehn
How far is it?	**Hur långt är det?**
	heur loangt air dee
Where can I buy tickets?	**Var kan jag köpa biljetter?**
	vahr kan yahg <u>chur</u> • pa bil • <u>yeht</u> • tehr

One-way [single]/ round-trip [return].	**Enkel/Retur.** *ehng • kehl/reh • teur*
How much does it cost?	**Hur mycket kostar det?** *heur mew • ker kos • tar dee*
Are there any discounts?	**Finns det några rabatter?** *fihns dee noa • gra ra • bat • ehr*
Which gate?	**Vid vilken gate?** *veed vihl • kehn gayt*
Which line?	**Vilken kö?** *vihl • kehn kur*
Which platform?	**Vilken plattform?** *vihl • kehn plat • fohrm*
Where can I get a taxi?	**Var kan jag få tag på en taxi?** *vahr kan yahg foa tahg poa ehn tax • ee*
Please take me to this address.	**Var snäll och kör mig till denna address.** *vahr snehl ohk churr may tihl deh • na ad • rehs*
Where can I rent a car?	**Var kan jag hyra en bil?** *vahr kan yahg hew • ra ehn beel*
I'd like a map.	**Jag skulle vilja ha en karta.** *Yahg skuh • ler vihl • ya hah ehn kahr • ta*

TICKETS

When is...to	**När går...till Uppsala?** *nair goar...tihl uhp • sah • la Uppsala?*
the (first) bus	**(första) bussen** *(furs • ta) buhs • ehn*

the (next) flight	**(nästa) flyg**	
	(nehs • ta) flewg	
the (last) train	**(sista) tåget**	
	(sihs • ta) toa • geht	
Where can I buy tickets?	**Var kan jag köpa biljetter?**	
	vahr kan yahg chur • pa bihl • yeht • er	
One ticket/Two tickets, please.	**En biljett/Två biljetter, tack.**	
	ehn bil • yet/tvoa bil • yeht • er tak	
For today/tomorrow.	**Till dagens/imorgon.**	
	tihl dah • gens/ee • mo • ron	
…ticket.	**…biljett.**	
	…bihl • yeht	
A one-way [single]	**En enkel**	
	ehn ehng • kehl	
A return-trip	**En retur**	
	ehn reh • teur	
A first class	**En första klass**	
	ehn furr • sta klas	
A business class	**En i affärsklass**	
	Ehn ee a • fairs • klas	
An economy class	**En turist klass**	
	ehn tuh • rihst klas	
How much does it cost?	**Hur mycket kostar det?**	
	heur mew • ker kos • tar dee	
Is there a discount for…?	**Blir det rabatt för…?**	
	bleer dee ra • bat furr…	
children	**barn**	
	bahrn	
students	**studerande**	
	steu • dee • ran • der	
senior citizens	**pensionärer**	
	pan • shoa • nair • ehr	
tourists	**turister**	
	tuh • rihst • ehr	

The express bus/ express train, please.	**Expressbussen/expresståget, tack.** *Ehx • prehs • buhs • ehn/ ehx • prehs • toa • geht, tak*
The local bus/train, please.	**Lokalbussen/tåget, tack.** *Loh • kahl • buhs • en/toa • geht, tak*
I have an e-ticket.	**Jag har en e-biljett.** *yahg hahr ehn ee • bihl • yet*
Can I buy a ticket on the bus/train?	**Kan jag köpa en biljett på bussen/ tåget?** *kan yahg chur • pa ehn bihl • yeht poa bus • ehn/toa • geht*
Do I have to stamp the ticket before boarding?	**Ska jag stämpla biljetten innan jag går ombord?** *Skah yahg stehm • pla bil • yet • ehn • ihn • ahn • yahg • goar • ohm • bohrd*
How long is this ticket valid?	**Hur länge gäller denna biljett?** *Heur lehng • er yeh • lehr deh • na bihl • yet*
Can I return on the same ticket?	**Kan jag åka tillbaka med samma biljett?** *Kahn yahg oak • ha tihl • bah • ka mehd sam • a bihl • yet*
I'd like to…my reservation.	**Jag skulle vilja…min bokning.** *Yahg skuh • ler vihl • ya…mihn boak • nihng*
cancel	**avbeställa** *afv • beh • steh • la*
change	**ändra** *ehn • dra*
confirm	**bekräfta** *beh • krehf • ta*

AIRPORT TRANSFER

How much is a taxi to the airport?	**Vad kostar en taxi till flygplatsen?** *Vahd <u>kos</u>•tar ehn <u>tax</u>•ee tihl <u>fle</u>wg•plat•sehn*
To...Airport, please.	**Till...Flygplats, tack.** *tihl...<u>fle</u>wg•plats tak*
My airline is...	**Mitt flygbolag är...** *miht <u>fle</u>wg•boa•lahg air...*
My flight leaves at...	**Mitt flyg avgår klockan...** *miht flewg <u>afv</u>•**goar** <u>kloh</u>•kan...*
I'm in a rush.	**Jag har bråttom.** *yahg hahr <u>broa</u>•tohm*
Can you take an alternate route?	**Kan du köra någon annan väg?** *kan deu <u>chur</u>•ra <u>noa</u>•gohn <u>an</u>•nan vehg*
Can you drive faster/ slower?	**Kan du köra lite fortare/långsammare?** *kan deu <u>chur</u>•ra <u>lee</u>•ter <u>foar</u>•ta•rer/<u>loang</u>•sam•a•rer*

YOU MAY HEAR...

Vilket flygbolag reser du med? *<u>vihl</u>•keht <u>fle</u>wg•boa•lahg <u>ree</u>•sehr deu meed*	What airline are you flying?
Inrikes eller utrikes? *<u>in</u>•ree•kehs <u>ehl</u>•er <u>eut</u>•ree•kehs*	Domestic or International?
Vilken terminal? *<u>vihl</u>•kehn tehr•mee•<u>nahl</u>*	What terminal?

CHECKING IN

Where is check-in?	**Var är incheckningen?**	
	vahr air in • shehk • nihng • ehn	
My name is...	**Jag heter...**	
	yahg hee • ter...	
I'm going to...	**Jag ska resa till...**	
	yahg skah ree • sa tihl...	
I have...	**Jag har....**	
	Yahg hahr...	
one suitcase	**en resväska**	
	ehn rehs • vehs • ka	
two suitcases	**två resväskor**	
	tvoh rehs • vehs • kohr	
one piece of hand luggage	**ett handbagage**	
	eht hand • ba • gah • sh	
How much luggage is allowed?	**Hur mycket gratis bagage får man ha?**	
	heur mew • ker grah • tihs ba • goash foar man hah	
Is that pounds or kilos?	**Är det i pund eller kilo?**	
	Air deht ee pund ehl • er cheeh • loh	
Which terminal/ gate does flight... leave from?	**Vid vilken terminal/gate går flygnummer...?**	
	veed vihl • kehn tehr • mee • nahl/gayt goar flewg • nuhm • ehr...	
I'd like a window/ an aisle seat.	**Jag skulle vilja ha en fönsterplats/ plats i mittgången.**	
	yahg skuh • ler vihl • ya hah ehn furns • tehr • plats/plats ee miht • goang • ehn	
When do we leave/ arrive?	**När avgår vi/är vi framme?**	
	nair afv • goar vee/air vee fra • mer	

Is flight...delayed?	**Är det någon försening på flyg...?**
	air dee noa • gohn furr • seen • ihng poa
	flewg...
How late will it be?	**Hur försenat är det?**
	heur furr • seen • at air dee

YOU MAY SEE...

ANKOMST	arrivals
AVGÅNG	departures
BAGAGEUTLÄMNING	baggage claim
INRIKESFLYG	domestic flights
UTRIKESFLYG	international flights
CHECKA IN	check-in
CHECKA IN E-BILJETT	e-ticket check-in
AVGÅNGSGATER	departure gates

YOU MAY HEAR...

Nästa!
nehs • ta

Next!

Er biljett/Ert pass, tack.
eer bihl • yet/ eert pas tak

Your ticket/ passport, please.

Hur mycket bagage har du?
heur mew • ker ba • goash hahr deu

How much luggage do you have?

Du har övervikt.
deu hahr ur • vehr • vikt

You have excess luggage.

Det där är för tungt/för stort handbagage.
dee dair air furr teungt/furr stoart hand • ba • goash

That's too heavy/large for a carry-on [to carry on board].

Packade du väskorna själv?
pa • ka • der deu vehs • kohr • na shehlv

Did you pack these bags yourself?

Har någon gett er något att ta med?
hahr noa • gohn yeht eer noa • goht at tah meed

Did anyone give you anything to carry?

Töm era fickor, tack.
turm ee • ra fihk • ohr tak

Empty your pockets, please.

Ta av er skorna, tack.
ta afv eer skoar • na tak

Take off your shoes, please.

Nu är ni välkommna att borda flight nummer...
neu air nee vail • kohm • na at bohr • da flajt nuhm • ehr...

Now boarding flight...

LUGGAGE

Where is/are...?	**Var finns...?**
	vahr fihns...
the luggage carts [trolleys]	**bagagekärrorna**
	ba • goash • chair • ohr • na
the luggage lockers	**förvaringsskåpen**
	furr • vah • rihng • skoap • ehn
the baggage claim	**bagageutlämningen**
	ba • goash • eut • lehm • nihng • ehn
I've lost my baggage.	**Jag har förlorat mitt bagage.**
	yahg hahr furr • loa • rat miht ba • goash
My baggage has been stolen.	**Mitt bagage har blivit stulet.**
	miht ba • goash hahr blee • viht steu • leht
My suitcase was damaged.	**Min resväska blev skadad.**
	Mihn rees • vehs • ka bleev skah • dad

FINDING YOUR WAY

Where is...?	**Var finns...?**
	vahr fihns...
the currency exchange office	**växelkontoret**
	vehx • ehl • kohn • toar • eht
the car hire	**biluthyrningen**
	beel • eut • hewr • nihng • ehn
the exit	**utgången**
	eut • goang • ehn
the taxi	**taxin**
	tax • een
Is there...into town?	**Finns det...in till stan?**
	fihns dee...ihn tihl stahn
a bus	**en buss**
	ehn buhs

a train	**ett tåg**
	eht toag
a subway	**tunnelbana**
	tuh • nehl • bah • na

For Asking Directions, see page 64.

YOU MAY SEE...

PLATTFORM	platform
SPÅR	tracks
INFORMATION	information
BILJETTKONTOR	ticket office
ANKOMST	arrival
AVGÅNG	departure

TRAIN

How do I get to the train station?	**Hur kommer jag till järnvägsstationen?**
	heur koh • mehr yahg tihl yairn • vaigs • sta • shoa • nehn
How far is it?	**Hur långt är det?**
	heur loangt air dee
Where is/are...?	**Var finns...?**
	vahr fihns...
the ticket office	**biljettkontoret**
	bihl • yet • kohn • toar • eht
the luggage lockers	**förvaringsskåpen**
	furr • vah • rihng • skoap • ehn
the platforms	**plattformarna**
	plat • fohr • mar • na
Could I have a schedule [timetable], please?	**Kan jag få en tidtabell, tack?**
	kan yahg foa ehn teed • ta • behl tak

How long is the trip?	**Hur lång tid tar resan?**
	heur loang teed tahr ree•san
Is it a direct train?	**Är det ett direkttåg?**
	air deh•ta eht dihr•ekt•toag
Do I have to change trains?	**Behöver jag byta tåg?**
	beh•hur•vehr yahg bew•ta toag
Is the train on time?	**Är tåget i tid?**
	air toag•het ee tihd

For Time, see page 24.

i

Statens järnvägar or **SJ** (the Swedish State Railway) operates an extensive network covering the entire country, while also offering international connections to Oslo, Copenhagen and Berlin. The X2000 train, which reaches speeds up to 200 km/h, serves many of Sweden's greater cities and towns. Long-distance trains have restaurant cars and/or buffets, and there are also sleepers and couchettes for both first and second class. The system is reliable and comfortable, and offers a wide range of travel options with respect to schedule and cost. Discount tickets are available for young children, families, students and senior citizens. Special travel cards and programs are also available. On some trains, marked **R** or **IC**, you must reserve a seat by purchasing a **sittplatsbiljett** in addition to your travel ticket. For extraordinary scenery, try the northern **Inlandsbanan** (Inland Railway) service, which runs from Mora in Dalarna to Gällivare beyond the Arctic circle. The **Vildmarksexpressen** (Wilderness Express) has old 1930s coaches and a gourmet restaurant, and runs on the same line between Östersund and Gällivare, with stops and excursions.

DEPARTURES

Which platform does the train to…leave from?	**Vilken plattform går tåget till…från?**
	Vihl • kehn plat • fohrm goar tao • geht froan
When is the train to…?	**När går tåget till…?**
	nair goar toa • geht tihl…
Is this the right platform for…?	**Är det här rätta plattformen till…?**
	air dee hair reh • ta plat • fohr • mehn tihl…
Where is platform…?	**Var är plattform…?**
	vahr air plat • fohrm…
Where do I change for…?	**Var måste jag byta till…?**
	vahr mos • ter yahg bew • ta tihl…

ON BOARD

Can I sit here/open the window?	**Kan jag sitta här/öppna fönstret?**
	Kan yahg sihta hair/urp • na fuhns • streht
Is this seat taken?	**Är den här platsen upptagen?**
	air dehn hair plats • ehn uhp • tah • gehn
That's my seat.	**Det där är min plats.**
	dee dair air mihn plats
Here's my reservation.	**Här är min bokning.**
	Hair air meen boak • nihng

BUS

Where's the bus station?	**Var är bussterminalen?**
	vahr air bus • tehr • mih • nahl • ehn
How far is it?	**Hur långt är det?**
	heur loangt air dee
How do I get to…?	**Hur kommer jag till…?**
	heur koh • mehr yahg tihl…

Does the bus stop at...?	**Stannar bussen vid...?**
	stan • ar _buhs_ • en veed...
Could you tell me when to get off?	**Kan du tala om för mig när jag ska stiga av?**
	kan deu _tah_ • la ohm fur_r_ may nair yahg skah _stee_ • ga afv
Do I have to change buses?	**Behöver jag byta buss?**
	beh • _hur_ • vehr yahg _bew_ • ta buhs
Stop here, please.	**Stanna här, tack.**
	sta • na hair tak

For Tickets, see page 45.

YOU MAY HEAR...

Påstigning!	All aboard!
poa • steeg • nihng	
Biljetter, tack.	Tickets, please.
bihl • _yet_ • er tak	
Du måste byta i...	You have to change in...
deu _moss_ • ter _bew_ • ta ee...	
Nästa hållplats...	Next stop...
nehs • ta _hoal_ • plats...	

YOU MAY SEE...

BUSSHÅLLPLATS	bus stop
INGÅNG/UTGÅNG	enter/exit
STÄMPLA ER BILJETT	stamp your ticket

Public transportation in Sweden is an excellent and well-maintained system that includes **bussar** (buses), **tunnelbanan** (subways), **spårvagnar** (trams) and **tåg** (trains). All of these run frequently, usually between 5:00 a.m. and midnight on weekdays and a bit later on weekends. Most cities and towns have a bus system, though only a few have trams and subways. While it is possible to purchase single tickets for the different modes of public transportation, it is more cost efficient to purchase a card or set of tickets if you are going to be using a particular network frequently. Most major cities have websites that provide up to date information on routes, tickets and prices; many of the sites have English as a language option.

SUBWAY

Where's the nearest subway [underground] station?	**Var är närmaste tunnelbanestation?** *Vahr air _nair_ • mas • ter* *tuh • nehl • bah • neh • sta • _shoan_*
Which direction?	**Åt vilket håll?** *Oat vihl • keht hohl*
Can I have a map of the subway [underground], please?	**Kan jag få en tunnelbanekarta, tack?** *Kan yahg fo̱a ehn* *tuh • nehl • bah • neh • _kahr_ • ta tak*
Which line should I take for...?	**Vilken linje ska jag ta till...?** *_vihl_ • kehn leen • yeh skah yahg tah tlhl...*
Where do I change for...?	**Var måste jag byta till...?** *vahr _mos_ • ter yahg _bew_ • ta tihl...*

Is this the train to…?	**Är det här tåget till…?**
	air dee hair toa • geht tihl…
How many stops to…?	**Hur många hållplatser är det till…?**
	Heur moh • ngah hohl • plat • sehr air deht tihl…
Where are we?	**Var är vi?**
	vahr air vee

For Tickets, see page 45.

The subway in Stockholm is efficient and easy to use. It runs from 5:00 a.m. to midnight on weekdays. Tickets are valid for one hour from the time they are stamped and can be bought from ticket booths; discount cards can be purchased from **Pressbyrån** (a newsstand). Tickets can also be purchased at **SL Centers**, some tourist offices and certain grocery stores. The public transportation websites will have information on these retailers and businesses and what types of tickets they sell. Day and multi-day cards are also available. Subway and bus tickets in Stockholm are interchangeable.

YOU MAY SEE...

LIVBÅT	life boat
FLYTVÄST	life jacket
ACTIVERA HANDBROMSEN	use parking brake
LÄMNA INTE VÄRDESAKER I BILEN	do not leave valuables in your car

BOAT & FERRY

When is the car ferry to Gotland leaving?	**Hur dags går bilfärjan till Gotland?** *heur daks goar beel • fair • yan tihl goht • land*
Where are the life jackets?	**Var finns flytvästarna?** *vahr fihns flewt • vehs • tar • na*
Can I take my car?	**Kan jag ta med min bil?** *Kahn yahg tah mehd meen bihl*
Can I drive on to the ferry now?	**Får jag köra ombord nu?** *foar yahg chur • ra ohm bohrd neu*
What time is the next sailing?	**Hur dags går nästa?** *Heur daks goar nehs • ta*
Can I book a seat/cabin?	**Kan jag boka en plats/hytt?** *Kahn yahg boa • ka plats/hewt*
How long is the trip?	**Hur lång är resan?** *heur loang air ree • san*
Where should I park?	**Var ska jag parkera?** *vahr skah yahg par • kee • ra*

ℹ️

Regular boat and ferry services, carrying cars and passengers, link Sweden to neighboring countries such as Norway, Denmark and Germany as well as to the U.K. Ferry services from Stockholm to the vacation destinations of Åland and Gotland in the Baltic Sea are very popular, as are ferries to Finland, Estonia and Latvia. Not to be missed are the ferry and steamer trips from Stockholm to the many surrounding islands, known as **Skärgården** (the Archipelago).

TAXI

Where can I get a taxi?	**Var kan jag få tag på en taxi?**
	vahr kan yahg foa tahg poa ehn tax • ee
I'd like a taxi now/for tomorrow at…	**Jag skulle vilja ha en taxi nu/imorgon klockan…**
	yahg skuh • ler vihl • ya hah ehn tax • ee neu/ee • mo • ron kloh • kan…
Can you send a taxi?	**Kan du skicka en taxi?**
	Kahn deu shih • ka ehn tax • ee
Do you have the number for a taxi?	**Har du numret till taxi?**
	Hahr deu nuhm • reht tihl tax • ee
Pick me up at… (place/time)	**Hämta mig vid/klockan…**
	hehm • ta may veed/kloh • kan…
I'm going to…	**Jag ska resa till…**
	yahg skah ree • sa tihl…
this address	**denna adress**
	deh • na ad • rehs
the airport	**flygplatsen**
	flewg • plat • sehn
the train station	**järnvägsstationen**
	yairn • vaigs • sta • shoa • nehn
I'm late.	**Jag är sen.**
	yahg air seen
Can you drive faster/ slower?	**Kan du köra fortare/långsammare?**
	Kan deu chur • ra fohrt • a • rer/ loang • sam • a • rer
Stop/Wait here.	**Stanna/Vänta här.**
	sta • na/vehn • ta hair
How much?	**Hur mycket kostar det?**
	heur mew • ker kos • tar dee
You said it would cost…kronor.	**Du sa att det skulle kosta…kronor.**
	deu sah at dee skuh • ler kos • ta… kroa • nohr

Keep the change.	**Behåll växeln.**
	be • hoal vehx • ehln
A receipt, please.	**Kvittot, tack.**
	kvih • tot tak

Taxis can be found at stands marked **Taxi.** You can also flag down a taxi in the street, especially near hotels and bus and train stations. Calling a taxi by phone is a third option; numbers are available from your concierge or a local phone book. The sign **Ledig** (free), when lit, indicates that the taxi is available.

YOU MAY HEAR...

Vart vill du åka?	Where to?
vart vihl deu oa • ka	
Vilken adress?	What's the
vihl • kehn ad • rehs	address?

BICYCLE & MOTORBIKE

I'd like to hire...	**Jag skulle vilja hyra...**
	yahg skuh • ler vihl • ya hew • ra...
a bicycle	**en cykel**
	ehn sew • kehl
a moped	**en moped**
	ehn moh • peed
a motorbike	**en motorcykel**
	ehn moa • tohr • sew • kehl

How much per day/week?	**Hur mycket kostar det per dag/vecka?**
	heur <u>mew</u>•ker kos•tar dee pair dahg/veh•ka
Can I have a helmet/lock?	**Kan jag få en hjälm/ett cykelås?**
	kan yahg foa ehn yehlm/eht <u>sew</u>•kehl•loas

YOU MAY HEAR...

Har du ett internationellt körkort?	Do you have an
hahr deu eht in•tehr•na•shoa•<u>nehlt</u> <u>churr</u>•koart	international driver's license?
Kan jag få se ert pass, tack?	May I see your
kan yahg foa see eert pas tak	passport, please?
Vill du ha en försäkring?	Do you want
vil deu hah ehn furr•<u>sair</u>•krihng	insurance?
Det blir en handpenning på...	There is a
dee bleer ehn <u>hand</u>•peh•nihng poa...	deposit of...
Underteckna här, tack.	Please sign
<u>uhn</u>•der•tehk•<u>na</u> hair tak	here.

CAR HIRE

Where can I hire a car?	**Var kan jag hyra en bil?**
	vahr kan yahg <u>hew</u>•ra ehn beel
I'd like to hire...	**Jag skulle vilja hyra...**
	yahg <u>skuh</u>•ler vihl•ya <u>hew</u>•ra...
a cheap/small car	**en billig/liten bil**
	en bihl•eeg/lee•tehn beel
a 2-/4-door car	**en bil med två/fyra dörrar**
	ehn beel meed tvoa/<u>few</u>•ra <u>dur</u>•rar

an automatic/ manual car	**en bil med automatväxel/ manuell**
	ehn beel meed ah • toa • maht • vehx • ehl/ mah • nuh • ehl
a car with air-conditioning	**en bil med luftkonditionering**
	ehn beel meed luhft • kohn • dee • shoa • neer • ihng
a car seat	**en bilbarnstol**
	ehn beel • barn • stoal
How much does it cost...?	**Hur mycket kostar det...?**
	heur mew • ker kos • tar dee...
per day/week	**per dag/vecka**
	pair dahg/veh • ka
per kilometer	**per kilometer**
	pair chee • loh • mee • ter
How much does it cost...?	**Hur mycket kostar det...?**
	heur mew • ker kos • tar dee...
for unlimited mileage	**för obegränsade mil**
	furr oa • beh • grehn • sa • deh • meel
with insurance	**med försäkring**
	meed furr • sair • krihng
Are there any special weekend rates?	**Har ni särskilda helgrabatter?**
	hahr nee sair • shihl • da hely • ra • bat • ehr

FUEL STATION

Where's the next fuel station, please?	**Ursäkta, var är närmaste bensinstation?**
	eur • shehk • ta vahr air nair • mas • the behn • seen • sta • shoan
Fill it up, please.	**Fyll tanken, tack.**
	feyl tan • kehn tak
...liters, please.	**...liter, tack.**
	...lee • tehr tak

I'll pay in cash/by credit card.	**Jag betalar kontant/med kreditkort.** *Yahg beh • tah • lar kohn • tant/meed kreh • deet • koart*

YOU MAY SEE...

VANLIG	regular
PREMIUM	premium [super]
DIESEL	diesel

ASKING DIRECTIONS

Is this the road to...?	**Är det här vägen till...?** *air dee hair vair • gehn tihl...*
How far is it to...?	**Hur långt är det till...?** *heur loangt air dee tihl...*
Where's...?	**Var ligger...?** *vahr lih • gehr...*
...Street	**...gata** *...gah • ta*
this address	**denna adress** *deh • na ad • rehs*
the highway [motorway]	**motorvägen** *moa • tohr • vair • gehn*
Can you show me on the map?	**Kan du visa mig på kartan?** *kan deu vee • sa may poa kahr • tan*
I'm lost.	**Jag har kommit vilse.** *yahg hahr koh • miht vihl • ser*

YOU MAY HEAR...

rakt fram	straight ahead
rahkt fram	
till vänster	on/to the left
tihl <u>vehn</u> • stehr	
till höger	on/to the right
tihl <u>hur</u> • gehr	
i/runt hörnan	on/around the
ee/ruhnt <u>hur</u> • nan	corner
mitt emot	opposite
miht ee • <u>mo</u>at	
bakom	behind
<u>bah</u> • kohm	
bredvid	next to
<u>breh</u> • veed	
efter	after
<u>ehf</u> • tehr	
norr/söder	north/south
nohr/<u>sur</u> • dehr	
öster/väster	east/west
<u>urs</u> • tehr/<u>vehs</u> • tehr	
vid trafikljusen	at the traffic
veed tra • <u>feek</u> • yeus • ehn	light
vid avfarten	at the exit
veed <u>afv</u> • far • tehn	

YOU MAY SEE...

STOP	**STOPP**	stop
	LÄMNA FÖRETRÄDE	give way
	PARKERING FÖRBJUDEN	no parking
	FARLIG KURVA	dangerous curve
	ENKELRIKTAT	one way
	INGEN INFART	no entry
	OMKÖRNING FÖRBJUDEN	no passing
	U-SVÄNG FÖRBJUDEN	no U-turn
	ÖVERGÅNGSSTÄLLE FÖR FOTGÄNGARE	pedestrian crossing

PARKING

Can I park here? **Får jag parkera här?**
foar yahg par • kee • ra hair

Is there a parking lot [car park] nearby? **Finns det en parkeringsplats i närheten?**
fihns dee ehn par • kee • rihngs • plats ee nair • hee • tehn

Where's…?	**Var ligger…?**
	Vahr lih • gehr…
the parking garage	**parkeringshuset**
	par-kee • rihngs • huhseht
the parking meter	**parkeringsautomaten**
	par • kee • rihngs ah • toa • mah • tehn
How much does it cost…?	**Hur mycket koster det…?**
	heur mew • ker kos • tar dee…
per hour	**per timme**
	pair tihm • er
per day	**per dag**
	pair dahg
overnight	**över natten**
	ur • vehr na • tehn

Street parking, parking lots and, in some cases, parking garages will be available in most of Sweden's cities and larger towns. Street parking is generally metered in city centers and downtown areas. A blue circular sign with a red slash tells you where parking is prohibited. There will be signs indicating whether or not parking is free. In places where parking is metered, a ticket allowing you to park for a specific period of time will need to be purchased. If this is the case, tickets can be purchased from a **biljettautomat** (ticket machine). You pay for the amount of time you want to park and then place the ticket on the driver's side of the car, on the dashboard, so that the ticket is in plain sight. In some cases, parking may be free, and there will be signs posted with time limits, usually two or three hours.

BREAKDOWN & REPAIR

My car broke down/ won't start.	**Min bil har gått sönder/startar inte.** *min beel hahr goat surn • dehr/star • tar in • ter*
Can you fix it today?	**Kan ni laga den idag?** *kan nee lah • ga dehn ee • dahg*
When will it be ready?	**När blir den färdig?** *nair bleer dehn fair • dihg*
How much?	**Hur mycket kostar det?** *heur mew • ker kos • tar dee*
I have a puncture/ flat tyre (tire).	**Jag har punktering.** *Yahg hahr puhng • teh • rihng*

ACCIDENTS

There's been an accident.	**Det har hänt en olycka.** *dee hahr hehnt ehn oa • lew • ka*
Call an ambulance/ the police.	**Ring efter en ambulans/polisen.** *rihng ehf • ter ehn am • beu • lans/ poa • lee • sehn*

PLACES TO STAY

NEED TO KNOW

Can you recommend a hotel in...?	**Kan du rekommendera ett hotel i...?**
	kan deu reh • koh • mehn • dee • ra eht hoh • tehl ee...
I have a reservation.	**Jag har bokat rum.**
	yahg hahr boa • kat ruhm
My name is...	**Jag heter...**
	yahg hee • tehr...
Do you have a room...?	**Har ni ett ledigt rum...?**
	hahr nee eht lee • dihgt ruhm...
for one/two	**för en person/två personer**
	furr ehn pehr • shoan/tvoa pehr • shoan • ehr
with a bathroom	**med badrum**
	meed bahd • ruhm
with air-conditioning	**med luftkonditionering**
	meed luhft • kohn • dee • shoa • neer • ihng
For tonight.	**För ikväll.**
	furr ee • kvehl
For two nights.	**För två nätter.**
	furr tvoa neh • tehr
For one week.	**För en vecka.**
	furr ehn veh • ka
How much?	**Hur mycket kostar det?**
	heur mew • ker kos • tar dee

Do you have anything cheaper?	**Har ni någonting billigare?** *hahr nee noa • gohn • tihng bihl • ee • ga • rer*
When's check-out?	**När måste vi checka ut?** *nair mos • ter vee sheh • ka eut*
Can I leave this in the safe?	**Kan jag lämna detta i kassaskåpet?** *Kan yahg lehm • na deh • ta ee ka • sah • skoa • peht*
Could we leave our baggage here until…?	**Kan vi lämna vårt bagage här till klockan…?** *kan vee lehm • na voart ba • goash hair tihl kloh • kan…*
Could I have the bill/ receipt, please?	**Kan jag få räkningen/kvittot, tack?** *Kan yahg foa rairk • nihng • en/kvih • toht tak*
I'll pay in cash/by credit card.	**Jag betalar kontant/med kreditkort.** *Yahg beh • tah • lar kohn • tant/meed kreh • deet • koart*

SOMEWHERE TO STAY

Can you recommend a hotel in...?	**Kan du rekommendera ett hotel i...?** *kan deu reh • koh • mehn • dee • ra eht hoh • tehl ee...*
a hostel	**ett vandrarhem** *eht vand • rar • hehm*
a campsite	**en kampingplats** *ehn kam • pihng • plats*
a bed and breakfast	**rum med frukost** *ruhm mehd fruh • kohst*
What is it near?	**Vad finns det i närheten?** *vahd fihns dee ee nair • hee • tehn*
How do I get there?	**Hur kommer jag dit?** *heur koh • mehr yahg deet*

AT THE HOTEL

I have a reservation.	**Jag har bokat rum.** *yahg hahr boh • kat ruhm*
My name is...	**Jag heter...** *yahg hee • tehr...*
Do you have a room...?	**Har ni ett rum...?** *hahr nee eht ruhm...*
with a bathroom/ shower	**med bad/dusch** *meed bahd/deush*
with air-conditioning	**med luftkonditionering** *meed luhft • kohn • dee • shoa • neer • ihng*
that's smoking/ non-smoking	**för rökare/icke-rökare** *furr rur • kah • rer/ ih • keh rur • ka • rer*
For tonight.	**För ikväll.** *furr ee • kvehl*

YOU MAY HEAR...

Ert pass/kreditkort, tack.
ehrt pas/ kreh • deet • koart tak

Your passport/ credit card, please.

Kan du fylla i den här blanketten.
kan deu few • la ee dehn hair blan • keh • tehn

Please fill out this form.

Skriv under här.
skreev uhn • der hair

Sign here.

For two nights.	**För två nätter.**	
	furr tvoa neh • tehr	
For one week.	**För en vecka.**	
	furr ehn veh • ka	
Does the hotel have...?	**Finns det...på hotellet?**	
	fihns dee...poa hoh • tehl • eht	
a computer	**en dator**	
	ehn dah • tohr	
an elevator [lift]	**en hiss**	
	ehn hihs	
(wireless) internet service	**(trådlös) internet**	
	(troad • lurs) in • tehr • net	
room service	**rumservice**	
	ruhm • sehr • vihs	
a pool	**en simbassäng**	
	ehn sihm • ba • sehng	
a gym	**ett gym**	
	eht ym	
I need...	**Jag behöver...**	
	yahg beh • hur • vehr...	
an extra bed	**en extra säng**	
	ehn ehx • tra sehng	

a cot	**en tältsäng**
	ehn tehlt • sehng
a crib	**en barnsäng**
	ehn bahrn • sehng

For Numbers, see page 22.

PRICE

How much per night/week?	**Vad kostar det per natt/vecka?**
	Vahd kos • tar dee pair nat/veh • ka
Does the price include breakfast/sales tax [VAT]?	**Ingår frukost/moms i priset?**
	ihn • goar fruh • kohst/mohms ee pree • seht
Are there any discounts?	**Ger ni rabatter?**
	Yehr nee ra • bat·ehr

PREFERENCES

Can I see the room?	**Kan jag se rummet?**
	Kan yahg seh ruhm • eht
I'd like a...room.	**Jag skulle vilja ha ett...rum.**
	Yahg skuh • ler vihl • ya hah eht ...ruhm
better	**bättre**
	beh • treh
bigger	**större**
	stuh • reh
cheaper	**billigare**
	bihl • ee • ga • rer
quieter	**tystare**
	tews • tah • rer
I'll take it.	**Ja tar det.**
	Yahg tahr deht
No, I won't take it.	**Nej, jag tar inte det.**
	Nay, yahg tahr deht in • ter

There is a wide range of places to stay in Sweden, from luxury to budget. Budget options include **privatrum** (private rooms), much like bed and breakfasts, or **stugor** (cabins) and **lägenheter** (apartments). Cabins and apartments are usually rented out on a weekly basis, but one- or two-night stays may also be an option. Information can be found at the local tourist office; you may also see signs along the road indicating that there is a vacancy in a cabin nearby. Motorists can look for **motel** (motels); these are reasonably priced with restaurants and car-friendly facilities. When looking for somewhere to stay in university towns such as Stockholm, Göteborg or Lund, staying at a **sommarhotel** (summer hotel) can be a good choice. Student dormitories are open to tourists in the summer and are a good option if you are traveling in a group. Families can enjoy a **familjehotell** (a family hotel), which has special rates for groups sharing the same room (three to six beds). These only operate during the summer months. All-inclusive accommodation is also available in the form of a **turisthotell** (tourist hotel) or **pensionat** (boarding house). These are clean and comfortable hotels or guesthouses that are often found at summer resorts and winter sport areas. Sweden also offers first class and deluxe hotels, usually found in larger cities and towns. Prices and amenities vary but the standards are usually high. Breakfast is usually included. When booking somewhere to stay during the summer months and high tourist season it is important to book in advance.

QUESTIONS

Where's...?	**Var ligger...?**
	vahr lih•gehr...
the bar	**baren**
	bah•rehn
the bathroom	**toaletten**
[toilet]	*toa•ah•leh•tehn*
the elevator [lift]	**hissen**
	his•ehn
Can I have...?	**Kan jag få...?**
	kan yahg foa...
a blanket	**ett täcke**
	eht teh•ker
an iron	**ett strykjärn**
	eht strewk•yairn
the room key/	**rumsnyckeln/nyckelkortet**
key card	*Ruhms•new•kehl/new•kehl•koart*
a pillow	**en kudde**
	ehn keu•der
soap	**tvål**
	tvoal
toilet paper	**toalettpapper**
	toa•ah•leht•pa•pehr
a towel	**en handduk**
	ehn han•deuk
Can I use this	**Kan jag använda den här adaptern här?**
adapter here?	*kan yahg an•vehn•da dehn hair*
	a•dap•tern hair
How do I turn on the	**Hur tänder man lamporna?**
lights?	*heur tehn•der man lam•pohr•na*
Could you wake	**Kan ni väcka mig klockan...?**
me at...?	*kan nee veh•ka may kloh•kan...*

Could I have my things from the safe?	**Kan jag få mina saker från kassaskåpet?**
	kan yahg foa mee • na sah • ker froan ka • sa • skoa • peht
Is there any mail/a message for me?	**Finns det någon post/eht meddelande till mig?**
	fihns dee noa • gohn pohst/eht meed • deel • an • der tihl may
Do you have a laundry service?	**Har ni tvättservice?**
	hahr nee tveht • sehr • vihs

YOU MAY SEE...

TRYCK	push
DRAG	pull
WC	restroom [toilet]
DAMTOALETT	women's restroom
HERRTOALETT	men's restroom
DUSCH	shower
HISS	elevator [lift]
TRAPPOR	stairs
TVÄTT	laundry
VAR GOD STÖR EJ	do not disturb
BRANDUTGÅNG	fire door
NÖDUTGÅNG	emergency exit
TELEFONVÄCKNING	wake-up call

PROBLEMS

There's a problem.	**Jag har ett problem.** *yahg hahr eht proh • bleem*
I've lost my key/ key card.	**Jag har tappat bort min nyckel/mitt nyckelkort.** *yahg hahr ta • pat bort mihn new • kehl/ miht new • kehl • koart*
I've locked myself out of my room.	**Jag har låst ut mig ur rummet.** *yahg hahr loast eut may eur ruhm • eht*
There's no hot water/ toilet paper.	**Det finns inget varmvatten/ toalettpapper.** *dee fihns ihng • eht varmt • va • tehrn/ toa • ah • leht • pa • per*
The room is dirty.	**Rummet är smutsigt.** *ruhm • eht air smuht • siht*
There are bugs in our room.	**Det finns insekter på vårt rum.** *dee fihns ihn • sehk • tehr poa voart ruhm*
Can you fix…?	**Kan ni laga…?** *kan nee lah • ga…*
the air- conditioning	**luftkonditioneringen** *luhft • kohn • dee • shoa • neer • ihng • ehn*
the fan	**fläkten** *flehk • tehn*
the heating	**värmen** *vair • mehn*
the light	**lampan** *lahm • pan*
the TV	**teven** *teh • veen*
the toilet	**toaletten** *toa • ah • leh • tehn*

I'd like to move to another room.	**Jag skulle vilja flytta till ett annat rum.**
	yahg skuh • ler vihl • ya flew • ta tihl eht an • at ruhm
...is/are broken.	**...är trasig.**
	...air trah • sihg

Throughout Sweden the current is 230-volt, 50-cycle AC. If you bring your own electrical appliances, buy a continental adapter plug (round pins) before leaving home. You may also need a transformer appropriate to the wattage of the appliance.

CHECKING OUT

When do we need to check out?	**När måste vi checka ut?**
	nair mos • ter vee sheh • ka eut
Could we leave our baggage here until...?	**Kan vi lämna vårt bagage här till klockan...?**
	kan vee lehm • na voart ba • goash hair tihl kloh • kan...
Can I have an itemized bill/receipt?	**Kan jag få en specificerad räkning/ett specificerad kvitto?**
	kan yahg foa ehn speh • seh • fee • ee • rad rairk • ning/eht speh • seh • fee • ee • rad kvih • toh
I think there's a mistake in this bill.	**Jag tror det måste vara fel på notan.**
	Yahg troar dee mos • ter vah • ra feel poa noa • tan.
I'll pay in cash/by credit card.	**Jag betalar kontant/med kreditkort.**
	Yahg beh • tah • lar kohn • tant/meed kreh • deet • koart

A service charge as well as **moms** (sales tax) is
included in hotel and restaurant bills, but you are expected
to round up a restaurant bill to the nearest **krona**. Tipping
is generally not expected, but it's always appreciated if
the service has been exceptionally good. It is customary to
give a small tip to hairdressers, barbers, taxi drivers and
porters.

RENTING

I've reserved an apartment/a room.	**Jag har bokat en lägenhet/ett rum.** *Yahg hahr boh•kat ehn lair•gehn•heet/ eht ruhm*
My name is...	**Jag heter...** *yahg hee•tehr...*
Can I have the key/ key card?	**Kan jag få nyckeln/nyckelkortet?** *kan yahg foa new•kehln/ new•kehl•koar•teht*
Are there...?	**Finns det...?** *fihns dee...*
dishes	**porslin** *poarsh•leen*
pillows	**kuddar** *keu•dar*
sheets	**lakan** *lah•kan*
towels	**handdukar** *han•deu•kar*
utensils	**bestick** *beh•stihk*

When do I put out the bins/recycling?	**När ska jag ställa ut soporna/återvinning?**
	nair skah yahg steh • la eut soa • pohr • na/oat • ehr • vihn • ing
...has broken down.	**...har gått sönder.**
	...hahr goat surn • dehr
How does...work?	**Hur fungerar...?**
	heur fuhn • geh • rar...
the air-conditioner	**luftkonditioneringen**
	luhft • kohn • dee • shoa • neer • ihng • ehn
the dishwasher	**diskmaskinen**
	dihsk • ma • shee • nehn
the freezer	**frysen**
	frew • sen
the heater	**värmeelementet**
	vair • meh • ehl • eh • mehn • teht
the microwave	**mikrovågsugnen**
	mik • roh • voags • eung • nehn
How does...work?	**Hur fungerar...?**
	heur fuhn • geh • rar...
the refrigerator	**kylskåpet**
	kewl • skoa • peht
the stove	**spisen**
	spee • sehn
the washing machine	**tvättmaskinen**
	tveht • mah • shee • nehn

DOMESTIC ITEMS

I'd like...	**Jag skulle vilja ha...**
	yahg skuh • ler vihl • ya hah...
an adapter	**en adapter**
	ehn a • dap • tehr
aluminum	**aluminiumfolie**
	ah • leu • mee • nee • um • foh • lyer foil

a bottle opener	**en flasköppnare**
	ehn flask • urp • na • rer
a broom	**en sopborste**
	ehn sop • borsh • ter
a can opener	**en konservöppnare**
	ehn kohn • serv • urp • na • rer
cleaning supplies	**städutrustning**
	staird • eut • reust • nihng
a corkscrew	**en korkskruv**
	ehn kohrk • skreuv
detergent	**tvättmedel**
	tveht • mee • dehl
dishwashing liquid	**diskmedel**
	disk • mee • dehl
bin bags	**soppåsar**
	sop • poa • sar
a light bulb	**en glödlampa**
	ehn glurd • lam • pa
matches	**tändstickor**
	tehnd • stih • kohr
a mop	**en skurmopp**
	ehn skewr • mop
napkins	**pappersservetter**
	pa • pers • sahr • veh • ter
plastic wrap [cling film]	**plastfolie**
	plast • foh • lyer
a plunger	**en vaskrensare**
	ehn vask • rehn • sa • rer
scissors	**en sax**
	ehn sax
a vacuum cleaner	**en dammsugare**
	ehn damm • seu • ga • rer

For In the Kitchen, see page 199.

If you are looking for something comfortable and reasonably priced, **Svenska Turistföreningen** or **STF** (the Swedish Tourist Club) is an excellent place to start. Here you can search for accommodations such as **vandrarhem** (youth hostels). If you are a member of **STF** or Hostelling International you get a member discount. Generally, room options include dormitory style rooms, split male and female, as well as smaller private rooms or family rooms. You are usually expected to bring your own towels and sheets as these usually are not provided, but can be rented. Shared kitchen facilities are often available, so that you can buy food at the local supermarket and prepare your own meals. Some hostels offer breakfast.

AT THE HOSTEL

Do you have any places left for tonight?	**Finns det några lediga platser ikväll?**
	*fihns d**ee** <u>noa</u> • gra <u>lee</u> • dih • ga <u>plats</u> • ehr ee • <u>kvehl</u>*
Can I have…?	**Kan jag få…?**
	kan yahg foa…
a single/double room	**ett enkelrum/dubbelrum**
	eht <u>hng</u> • kehl • ruhm/<u>duh</u> • behl • ruhm
a blanket	**ett täcke**
	eht <u>tehk</u> • er
a pillow	**en kudde**
	ehn <u>keu</u> • der
sheets	**lakan**
	<u>lah</u> • kan
a towel	**en handduk**
	*ehn <u>han</u> • d**eu**k*

What time are the doors locked?	**När stängs ytterdörrarna?**
	nair stehngs <u>ew</u> • ter • dur • ar • na
Do I need a membership card?	**Behöver jag medlemskort?**
	beh • hur • vehr yahg mehd • lehms • koart
Here's my international student card.	**Här är mitt internationella studentkort.**
	hair air miht in • tehr • na • shoa • nehl • ah stuh • dehnt • koart

GOING CAMPING

Can I camp here?	**Får man tälta här?**
	foar man <u>tehl</u> • ta hair
Is there a campsite near here?	**Finns det en campingplats i närheten?**
	fihns dee ehn <u>kam</u> • pihng • plats ee nair • hee • tehn
What is the charge per day/week?	**Vad kostar det per dag/vecka?**
	vahd <u>kos</u> • tar dee pair dahg/<u>veh</u> • ka
Are there…?	**Finns det…?**
	fihns dee…
cooking facilities	**kokmöjligheter**
	<u>koak</u> • mury • lihg • hee • tehr
electrical outlets	**nätuttag**
	<u>nairt</u> • eut • tahg
laundry facilities	**tvättmöjligheter**
	<u>tveht</u> • mury • lig • hee • tehr
showers	**dusch**
	deush
tents for hire	**tält för uthyrning**
	tehlt furr <u>eut</u> • hewr • nihng
Where can I empty the chemical toilet?	**Var kan jag tömma den kemiska toaletten?**
	vahr kan yahg <u>tur</u> • ma dehn sheh • mihs • ka toa • ah • <u>leh</u> • tehn

For Domestic Items, see page 80.

YOU MAY SEE...

DRICKSVATTEN	drinking water
INGEN CAMPING	no camping
INGEN GRILLNING	no barbeques
INGEN ÖPPEN ELD	no fires

COMMUNICATIONS

NEED TO KNOW

Where's an internet cafe?
Var finns det ett internetkafé?
vahr fihns dee eht
ihn • tehr • neht • ka • feh

Can I access the internet/check e-mail here?
Kan jag komma ut på internet/kola e-post här?
kan yahg koh • ma eut poa
ihn • tehr • neht/koa • la ee • pohst hair

How much per hour/half hour?
Hur mycket kostar det per timme/halvtimme?
heur mew • ker kos • tar dee pair
tihm • er/halv • tihm • er

How do I connect/log on?
Hur loggar jag in?
heur loh • gar yag ihn

Can I have a phone card?
Kan jag få ett telefonkort?
kan yahg foa eht teh • leh • foan • koart

Can I have your phone number?	**Kan jag få ditt telefonnummer?** *kan yahg foa diht* *teh•leh•**foan**•nuhm•ehr*
Here's my number/ e-mail address.	**Här är mitt nummer/min e-postadress.** *hair air miht **nuhm**•ehr/mihn* *ee•**pohst**•ad•rehs*
Call me.	**Var snäll och ring mig.** *vahr snehl ohk ring may*
E-mail me.	**Skicka en e-post till mig.** *shih•ka ehn ee•**pohst** tihl may*
Hello. This is…	**Hej. Det här är…** *hay dee hair air…*
I'd like to speak to…	**Jag skulle vilja tala med…** *yahg skuh•ler vihl•ya tah•la meed…*
Repeat that, please.	**Kan du upprepa det, tack.** *kan deu uhp•ree•pa dee tak*
I'll be in touch.	**Jag hör av mig snart.** *yahg hur afv may snahrt*
Goodbye.	**Hej då.** *hay doa*
Where is the post office?	**Var ligger posten?** *vahr lih•gehr pohs•tehn*
I'd like to send this to…	**Jag skulle vilja skicka det här till…** *yahg skuh•ler vihl•ya shih•ka dee hair tihl…*

ONLINE

Where's an internet cafe?	**Var finns det ett internetcafe?**
	vahr fihns deht eht
	ihn • tehr • neht • ka • feh
Does it have wireless internet?	**Finns det trådlös internet där?**
	fihns dee <u>troad</u> • lurs ihn • tehr • <u>neht</u> dair
What is the WiFi password?	**Vilket är WiFi-lösenordet?**
	vihl • keht wai • fai-lur • sehn • oarde
Is the WiFi free?	**Är WiFi gratis?**
	air wai • fain grah • tihs
Do you have bluetooth?	**Har ni blåtand?**
	hahr nee bloa • tand
How do I turn the computer on/off?	**Hur sätter jag på/stänger jag av datorn?**
	heur <u>seh</u> • tehr yahg poa/<u>stehng</u> • her yahg afv <u>dah</u> • torn
Can I print?	**Kan jag skriva ut?**
	*kan yahg <u>skree</u> • va **eu**t*
Can I…?	**Kan jag…?**
	kahn yahg…
access the internet	**gå ut på internet**
	goa eut poa ihn • tehr • neth

check my e-mail	**kolla min e-post**	
	kohla meen eh•pohst	
plug in/charge my laptop/iPhone/ iPad/BlackBerry?	**sätta i/ladda min laptop/iPhone/ iPad/BlackBerry**	
	sehta ih/ladha meen laptop/iPad/ BlackBerry	
access Skype?	**använda Skype**	
	an•vehn•a Skype	
How much per half hour/hour?	**Hur mycket kostar det per halvtimme/ timme?**	
	Heur mew•keh koh•star deht pehr halv•tihm•er/tih•mer	
How do I...?	**Hur gör man för att...?**	
	heur yurr man furr at...	
connect/ disconnect	**koppla upp/koppla ner**	
	kohp•la uhp/kohp•la nehr	
log on/off	**logga in/ut**	
	loh•ga ihn/eut	
type this symbol	**skriva in det här tecknet**	
	skree•va ihn dee hair tehk•neht	
What's your e-mail?	**Vad har du för e-postadress?**	
	vahd hahr deu furr ee•pohst•ad•rehs	
My e-mail is...	**Min e-postadress är...**	
	mihn ee•pohst•ad•rehs air...	
Do you have a scanner?	**Har ni en skanner?**	
	Hahr nee ehn ska•nehr	

SOCIAL MEDIA

Are you on Facebook/Twitter?	**Finns du på Facebook/Twitter?**	
	Fihns deu poa Facebook/Twitter	
What's your user name?	**Vilket användarnamn har du?**	
	Vihl•keht an•vehn•dar•namn hahr deu	
I'll add you as a friend.	**Jag lägger till dig som vän.**	
	yahg lehg•ehr tihl day sohm vehn	

I'll follow you on Twitter.	**Jag följer dig på Twitter.**
	Yahg fuhl•yehr day poa Twitter
Are you following…?	**Följer du…?**
	Fuhl•yehr deu…
I'll put the pictures on Facebook/Twitter.	**Jag lägger ut bilderna på Facebook/Twitter.**
	yahg lehg•ehr eut bihl•dehr•na poa Facebook/Twitter
I'll tag you in the pictures.	**Jag taggar bilderna.**
	yahg ta•gar bihl•dehr•na

YOU MAY SEE...

STÄNG	close
RADERA	delete
E-POST	e-mail
UTGÅNG	exit
HJÄLP	help
INSTANT MESSENGER	instant messenger
INTERNET	internet
LOGGA IN	login
NYTT MEDDELANDE	new message
AV/PÅ	on/off
ÖPPNA	open
SKRIV UT	print
SPARA	save
SKICKA	send
ANVÄNDARNAMN	username
LÖSENORD	password
TRÅDLÖS INTERNET	wireless internet

PHONE

A phone card/ prepaid phone please.	**Ett telefonkort, tack.** *eht teh • leh • foan • koart tak*
How much does it cost?	**Hur mycket kostar det?** *heur mew • ker kos • tar dee*
What's the area/ country code for...?	**Vad är riktnumret/landskoden till...?** *vahd air rikt • nuhm • reht/ lands • koa • dehn tihl...*
What's the number for Information?	**Vilket nummer är det till Nummerbyrån?** *vihl • keht nuhm • ehr air dee tihl nuhm • ehr • bew • roan*
I'd like the number for...	**Jag skulle vilja ha numret till...** *yahg skuh • ler vihl • ya hah nuhm • reht tihl...*
I'd like to call collect [reverse the charges].	**Jag vill ringa ett mottagaren-betalar-samtal.** *yahg vihl rihng • a eht moh • tah • ga • ren be • tah • lar-sam • tahl*
My phone doesn't work here.	**Min telefon fungerar inte här.** *mihn teh • leh • foan fuhn • geh • rar ihn • ter hair*
What network are you on?	**Vilket nätverk använder du?** *vihl • keht neht • vehrk an • vehn • der deu*
Is it 3G?	**Är det 3G?** *air deht treh • geh*
I have run out of credit/minutes.	**Jag har inte mer pengar/minuter på kortet.** *yahg hahr ihn • ther meer pehng • ar/ mih • nuh • tehr poa koart • eht*
Can I buy some credit?	**Kan jag fylla på kortet?** *kahn yahg fewlah poa koart • et*

Do you have a phone charger?	**Har du/ni en telefonladdare?**
	Hahr deu/nee ehn teh•leh•foan•lad•ar•eh
Can I have your number?	**Kan jag få ditt telefonnummer?**
	kan yahg foa diht teh•leh•foan•nuhm•ehr
Here's my number.	**Här är mitt nummer.**
	hair air miht nuhm•ehr
Please call me.	**Var snäll och ring mig.**
	vahr snehl ohk rihng may
Please text me.	**Var snäll och skicka ett sms till mig.**
	Vahr snehl ohk shih•ka eht ehs•ehm•ehs tihl may
I'll call you.	**Jag ringer dig.**
	yahg rihng•ehr day
I'll text you.	**Jag skickar ett sms till dig.**
	yahg shih•kar eht ehs•ehm•ehs tihl day

TELEPHONE ETIQUETTE

Hello. This is…	**Hej. Det här är…**
	hay dee hair air…
I'd like to speak to…	**Jag skulle vilja tala med…**
	yahg skuh•ler vihl•ya tah•la meed…
Extension…	**Anknytning…**
	an•knewt•nihng…
Speak louder/more slowly.	**Var snäll och tala högre/långsammare.**
	vahr snehl ohk tah•la hur•greh/ loang•sam•a•rer
Can you repeat that?	**Kan du upprepa det?**
	kan deu uhp•ree•pa pa dee
I'll call back later.	**Jag ringer senare.**
	yahg rihng•ehr see•na•rer
Goodbye.	**Hej då.**
	hay doa

YOU MAY HEAR...

Vem är det?	Who's calling?
vehm air dee	
Ett ögonblick.	One moment.
eht ur•gohn•blihk	
Tyvärr, är han/hon inte här.	I'm afraid he/she is not in.
tew•vair air hahn/hoan ihn•ter hair	
Han/Hon kan inte komma till telefonen.	He/She can't come to the phone.
hahn/hoan kan ihn•ter koh•ma tihl teh•leh•foan•ehn	
Vill du lämna ett meddelande?	Would you like to leave a message?
vihl deu lehm•na eht mee•dee•lan•der	
Ring tillbaka senare/om tio minuter.	Call back later/in 10 minutes.
rihng tihl•bah•ka see•na•rer/ohm tee•oah mih•neu•tehr	
Kan han/hon ringa upp dig?	Can he/she call you back?
kan hahn/ hoan rihng•a uhp day	
Vad är ditt telefonnummer?	What's your number?
vahd air dihtte•leh•foan•nuhm•her	

FAX

Can I send/receive a fax here?	**Kan man skicka/ta emot fax här?**
	kan man shih•ka/ta ee•moat fax hair
What's the fax number?	**Vad är ditt faxnummer?**
	vahd air diht fax•nuhm•ehr
Please fax this to...	**Var snäll och faxa det här till...**
	vahr snehl ohk fax•ah dee hair tihl...

To call the U.S. or Canada from Sweden, dial 00 + 1 +
area code + phone number. To call the U.K., dial 00 +
44 + area code (minus first 0) + phone number. Information
on area codes for Sweden and international dialing codes
can be found in the phone book and are usually available
at hotels and youth hostels. The emergency number in
Sweden is 112.

POST

Where's the post office/mailbox?	**Var ligger posten/postlådan?** *vahr lih • gehr pohs • tehn/pohst • loa • dan*
A stamp for this postcard/letter, please.	**Kan jag få ett frimärke till det här vykortet/brevet, tack.** *kan yahg foa eht free • mair • ker tihl dee hair vew • koar • teht/ bree • veht tak*
How much does it cost?	**Hur mycket kostar det?** *heur mew • ker kos • tar dee*
I want to send this package by airmail/ express.	**Jag vill skicka det här paketet med flygpost/express.** *yahg vihl shih • ka dee hair pa • kee • teht meed flewg • pohst/ehx • prehs*
The receipt, please.	**Kvittot, tack.** *kvih • toht tak*

YOU MAY HEAR...

Fyll i tulldeklarationen, tack.	Please fill out
fewl ee <u>tuhl</u> • deh • klar • a • <u>shoa</u> • nehn	the customs
tak	declaration
	form.
Vad är värdet?	What's the
vahd air <u>vair</u> • deht	value?
Vad finns inuti?	What's inside?
vahd fihns <u>ihn</u> • eu • <u>tee</u>	

Posten (the post office) is easy to find, just look
for the blue **Post** sign with a yellow horn. Mailboxes are
bright yellow. Business hours are 9:00 a.m. to 6:00 p.m.
and on Saturdays, until 1:00 p.m. Like many other stores
and business, you will need to take a number and wait
for it to be called or displayed on a screen before you
can be helped. Stamps can be purchased at **Pressbyrån**
(newsstand chain) as well as some grocery stores.

SIGHTSEEING

NEED TO KNOW

Where's the tourist information office?	**Var ligger turistinformationen?** *vahr <u>lih</u> • gehr teu • <u>rihst</u> • ihn • fohr • ma • <u>shoan</u> • ehn*
What are the main points of interest?	**Vad finns det för sevärdheter?** *vahd fihns dee furr <u>see</u> • vaird • hee • tehr*
Do you have tours in English?	**Finns det några turer på engelska?** *fihns dee <u>noa</u> • gra teu • rehr poa <u>ehng</u> • ehl • ska*
Can I have a map/ guide, please?	**Kan jag få en karta/guide, tack?** *kan yahg foa ehn <u>kahr</u> • ta/gujd tak*

TOURIST INFORMATION

Do you have any information on...?	**Har ni information om...?** *hahr nee ihn • for • ma • <u>shoan</u> om...*
Can you recommend...?	**Kan ni rekommendera...?** *kan nee reh • koh • mehn <u>dee</u> • ra...*

There are tourist information offices in all large
cities and towns. These are usually marked by a green
sign with an **I**. For general information, Sweden's official
tourism website is a good place to start. Here you can find
information on accommodation, attractions and activities
as well as cultural and historical information. Most cities
have their own tourist boards and websites, where you can
request brochures, maps and more prior to your arrival.
Also look for **Stockholmskortet** (the Stockholm Card) if
you will be spending several days in the city. For one fee,
you have access to musems, events and transportation
throughout the city. You can choose whether you want the
card for 24, 48 or 72 hours. The equivalent in Göteborg is
Göteborgs Passet.

a boat trip	**en båttur**
	ehn <u>boat</u> • teur
an excursion	**en rundtur**
	ehn <u>ruhnd</u> • teur
a sightseeing tour	**en sightseeingtur**
	ehn <u>sight</u> • see • ihng • teur

ON TOUR

I'd like to go on the tour to…	**Jag vill följa med på turen till…**
	yahg vihl <u>fur</u>l • ja meed p<u>oa</u> <u>teu</u> • ren tihl…
When's the next tour?	**När går nästa rundresa?**
	nair goar ne<u>h</u>sta ruhnd • rehsa
Are there tours in English?	**Finns det någon tur på engelska?**
	fihns d<u>ee</u> <u>noa</u> • gohn teur p<u>oa</u> <u>ehng</u> • ehl • ska

Is there an English-speaking guide/ audio guide?	**Finns det en engelsktalande guide/ ljudguide?**
	fihns deht ehn ehng • ehlsk • tah • lan • de gahyd/ aw • dee • oh gahyd
What time do we leave/return?	**När åker vi/kommer vi tillbaka?**
	nair oak • er vee/koh • mehr vee tihl • bah • ka
We'd like to have a look at...	**Vi skulle vilja se...**
	vee skuh • ler vihl • ya see...
Can we stop here...?	**Kan vi stanna här...?**
	kan vee sta • na hair...
to take photographs	**för att ta foton**
	furr at tah foa • tohn
to buy souvenirs	**för att köpa souvenirer**
	furr at chur • pa seu • veh • nee • rehr
to use the toilets	**för att gå på toaletten**
	furr at goa poa toa • ah • leh • tehn
Is there access for the disabled?	**Finns det tillgång för rörelsehindrade?**
	fihns dee tihl • goang furr rurr • ehl • ser • hihn • dra • der

For Tickets, see page 45.

SEEING THE SIGHTS

Where is...?	**Var ligger...?**
	vahr lih • gehr...
the battleground	**slagfältet**
	slahg • fehl • teht
the botanical garden	**botaniska trädgården**
	boa • tan • ihs • ska traird • goar • dehn
Where is...?	**Var ligger...?**
	vahr lih • gehr...
the castle	**slottet**
	sloht • eht

the downtown area	**centrum**
	sehn • truhm
the fountain	**fontänen**
	fohn • tairn • ehn
the library	**biblioteket**
	bihb • lee • oa • teek • eht
the market	**torget**
	tohr • yeht
the museum	**museet**
	muh • see • eht
the old town	**gamla stan**
	gam • la stahn
the opera house	**operan**
	oap • eh • ran
the palace	**slottet**
	sloht • eht
the park	**parken**
	park • ehn
the shopping area	**Et affärscentrumet**
	eht a • ffairs • sehn • truhm • eht
the town hall	**stadshuset**
	stads • heus • eht
Can you show me on the map?	**Kan du visa mig på kartan?**
	kan deu vee • sa may poa kahr • tan

It's...	**Det är...**
	det air...
amazing	**fantastiskt**
	fan • ta • stihskt
beautiful	**vackert**
	va • kehrt
boring	**trist**
	trihst
interesting	**intressant**
	in • treh • sant
magnificent	**storslaget**
	stoar • slahg • eht
romantic	**romantiskt**
	roh • man • tihskt
strange	**konstigt**
	kohn • stihgt
stunning	**förbluffande**
	furr·bluh·fahnder
terrible	**hemskt**
	hehmskt
ugly	**fult**
	feult
I (don't) like it.	**Jag tycker (inte) om den/det.**
	yahg tew • kehr (in • ter) ohm dehn/dee

For Asking Directions, see page 64.

RELIGIOUS SITES

Where is...?	**Var är...?**
	vahr air...
the cathedral	**domkyrkan**
	dohm • chewr • kahn
the church	**kyrkan**
	chewr • kan

the mosque	**moskén**
	mos • kehn
the shrine	**altaret**
	alt • a • reht
the synagogue	**synagogan**
	sihn • a • gohg • an
the temple	**templet**
	tehmp • leht
What time is mass/ the service?	**Hur dags är mässan/gudstjänsten?**
	heur daks air mehs • an/ geuds • tjain • stehn

LEISURE TIME

SHOPPING

NEED TO KNOW

Where is the market/ mall [shopping centre]?	**Var ligger orget/affärscentrumet?** *vahr lih • gehr tohr • yeht/ a • ffairs • sehn • truhm • eht*
I'm just looking.	**Jag tittar bara.** *yahg tih • tar bah • ra*
Can you help me?	**Kan du hjälpa mig?** *kan deu yehlp • a may*
I'm being helped.	**Jag får hjälp, tack.** *yahg foar yehlp tak*
How much does it cost?	**Hur mycket kostar det?** *heur mew • ker kos • tar det*
This/That one, thanks.	**Den här/där, tack.** *dehn hair/dair tak*
That's all, thanks.	**Det var allt, tack.** *dee vahr alt tak*
Where do I pay?	**Var kan jag betala?** *vahr kan yahg beh • tah • la*
I'll pay in cash/by credit card.	**Jag vill betala kontant/med kreditkort.** *yahg vihl beh • tah • la kohn • tant/meed kreh • deet • koart*
A receipt, please.	**Kvittot, tack.** *kvih • tot tak*

AT THE SHOPS

Where is...?	**Var finns...?** *vahr fihns...*

the antiques store	**antikaffären**
	an • teek • a • ffair • ehn
the bakery	**bageriet**
	bahg • eh • ree • eht
the bookstore	**bokhandeln**
	boak • han • dehln
the clothing store	**klädaffären**
	klaird • a • ffair • ehn
the delicatessen	**delikatessaffären**
	dehl • eh • ka • tehs • a • fair • ehn
the department store	**varuhuset**
	vahr • eu • heus • eht
the health food store	**hälsokostaffären**
	hehl • soa • kost • a • fair • ehn
the jeweler	**juveleraren**
	yeu • veh • lee • rar • ehn
the liquor store [off-licence]	**systembolaget**
	sews • teem • boa • lahg • eht
the market	**torget**
	tohr • yeht
the pastry shop	**konditoriet**
	kohn • deh • toh • ree • eht
the pharmacy [chemist]	**apoteket**
	a • poa • tee • keht
the produce [grocery] store	**livsmedelsaffären**
	lihvs • mee • dehls • a • fair • ehn
the shoe store	**skoaffären**
	skoa • a • fair • ehn
the shopping mall [shopping centre]	**affärscentrumet**
	a • ffairs • sehn • truhm • eht
the souvenir store	**souvenirbutiken**
	seu • veh • neer • buh • tee • kehn
the supermarket	**snabbköpet**
	snab • chur • peht

Although Sweden still has many small, specialty shops, **Köpcentrum** (malls) are becoming more and more common, especially in larger towns. Many chain and department stores, such as **Åhléns** and **Kappahl** and **Hennes & Mauritz**, have branches all over the country, all of which sell quality goods. In the well-established Stockholm department store **NK**, you can find almost anything, though it can be quite expensive. Designer goods can be found at **DesignTorget** in Stockholm. For traditional handicrafts look for signs with **hemslöjd** (handicraft); in Stockholm, these can be found at **Svensk Hemslöjd** and **Svenskt Hantverk** (traditional handicraft stores). Many towns have colorful markets, where you can buy anything from fresh fruit and vegetables to flowers and handicrafts. **Julmarknaden** (Christmas market) in Stockholm in the Old Town and **Skansen** (outdoor park and museum), are historic shopping areas.

Where is…?	**Var finns…?**
	vahr fihns…
the tobacconist	**tobaksaffären**
	toa • baks • a • ffair • ehn
the toy store	**leksaksaffären**
	leek • sahks • a • fair • ehn

ASK AN ASSISTANT

When do you open/ close?	**När öppnar/stänger ni?**
	nair uhp • nar/stehng • er nee
Where is…?	**Var finns…?**
	vahr fihns…

the cashier [cash desk]	**kassan** _kah_•san
the escalator	**rulltrappan** _ruhl_•tra•pan
the elevator [lift]	**hissen** _his_•ehn
the fitting room	**provrummet** _proav_•ruhm•eht
the store directory [guide]	**informationen** in•for•ma•_shoa_•nehn
Can you help me?	**Kan du hjälpa mig?** kan deu _yehl_•pa may
I'm just looking.	**Jag tittar bara.** yahg _tih_•tar _bah_•ra
I'm being helped.	**Tack, jag får hjälp.** tak yahg _foar_ yehlp
Do you have any...?	**Har ni några...?** hahr nee _noa_•gra...
Could you show me...?	**Kan du visa mig några...?** kan deu _vee_•sa may _noa_•gra...
Can you ship/ wrap it?	**Kan du skicka/slå in det?** kan deu _shih_•ka dee/_sloa_ ihn dee
How much does it cost?	**Hur mycket kostar det?** heur _mew_•kerht _kos_•tar dee
That's all, thanks.	**Det var allt, tack.** dee vahr alt tak

For Clothes & Accessories, see page 114.

PERSONAL PREFERENCES

I want something...	**Jag skulle vilja ha något...** yahg _skuh_•ler _vihl_•ya hah _noa_•goht...

YOU MAY HEAR...

Kan jag hjälpa er?
kan yahg yehl • pa her

Can I help you?

Ett ögonblick, tack.
eht ur • gohn • blihk tak

Just a moment, please.

Vad vill ni beställa?
vahd vihl nee beh • steh • la

What would you like?

Något annat?
noa • goht an • nat

Anything else?

---

cheap/expensive	**billigt/dyrt**
	bihl • igt/dewyt
larger/smaller	**större/mindre**
	sturr • er/mihn • drer
from this region	**från denna region**
	frohn deh • na regheoan
Is it real?	**Är den äkta?**
	air dehn aik • ta
Could you show me this/that?	**Kan du visa mig den här/där?**
	kan deu vee • sa may dehn hair/dair
That's not quite what I want.	**Det är inte riktigt vad jag vill ha.**
	dee air ihn • ter rihk • tikt vahd yahg vihl hah
I don't like it.	**Jag tycker inte om det.**
	yahg tew • kehr ihn • ter ohm dee
That's too expensive.	**Det är för dyrt.**
	dee air furr dewrt
I'd like to think about it.	**Jag behöver tänka på det.**
	Yahg beh • hur • vehr tehng • ka poa dee
I'll take it.	**Jag tar den.**
	yahg tahr dehn

YOU MAY SEE...

ÖPPET/STÄNGT	open/closed
STÄNGT FÖR LUNCH	closed for lunch
PROVRUM	fitting room
KASSÖR/KASSÖRSKA	cashier
ENDAST KONTANT	cash only
VI TAR KREDITKORT	credit cards accepted
AFFÄRSTID	business hours
UTGÅNG	exit

PAYING & BARGAINING

How much does it cost?	**Hur mycket kostar det?** *heur <u>mew</u>•ker <u>kos</u>•tar dee*
I'll pay...	**Jag betalar...** *yahg beh•<u>tah</u>•lar...*
in cash	**kontant** *kohn•<u>tant</u>*
by credit card	**med kreditkort** *meed kreh•<u>deet</u>•koart*
by traveler's check [cheque]	**med en resecheck** *meed ehn <u>ree</u>•seh•shehk*
The receipt, please.	**Kvittot, tack.** *<u>kvih</u>•toht tak*
That's too much.	**Det är för mycket.** *dee air furr <u>mew</u>•ker*
I'll give you...	**Jag kan ge er...** *yahg kan yee ehr...*

I only have…kronor. **Jag har bara…kronor.**
yahg hahr bah•ra…kroa•nohr

Is that your best price? **Är det ditt bästa pris?**
air deht diht beh•sta prihs

Can you give me a discount? **Kan du ge mig rabatt?**
kan deu yee may ra•bat

For Numbers, see page 22.

YOU MAY HEAR…

Hur vill ni betala? How are you
heur vihl nee beh•tah•la paying?

Ditt kreditkort har avvisats. Your credit card
diht kreh•dith•koart hahr ahv•veesahts has been
declined.

ID, tack. ID, please.
ee•deh, tak.

Vi tar inte kreditkort. We don't
Vee tahr ihnte kreh•diht•koart accept credit
cards.

Bara kontanter, tack. Cash only,
bah•ra kohn•tan•tehr tak please.

Har du mindre växel? Do you have
hahr deu mihn•drer vehx•ehl any smaller
change?

MAKING A COMPLAINT

I'd like...	**Jag skulle vilja...**
	yahg skuh • ler vihl • ya...
to exchange this	**byta den här**
	bew • ta dehn hair
to return this	**återlämna den här**
	oa • tehr • lehm • na dehn hair
a refund	**ha pengarna tillbaka**
	hah pehng • ar • na tihl • bah • ka
to see the manager	**få träffa butikschefen**
	foa treh • fa beu • teeks • sheef • ehn

SERVICES

Can you recommend...?	**Kan du rekommendera...?**
	kan deu reh • koh • mehn • dee • ra...
a barber	**en herrfrisör**
	ehn hair • fri • surr
a dry cleaner	**en kemtvätt**
	ehn shehm • tveht
a hairdresser	**en damfrisör**
	ehn dahm • free • surr
a laundromat [launderette]	**en snabbtvätt**
	ehn snab • tveht
a nail salon	**en nagelvårdssalong**
	ehn nah • gehl • voards • sa • loang
a spa	**ett spa**
	eht spah
a travel agency	**en resebyrå**
	ehn ree • seh • bew • rna
Can you...this?	**Kan ni...den här?**
	kan nee...dehn hair

alter	**ändra på**
	ehn • dra p**oa**
clean	**göra ren**
	yur • _ra reen_
mend	**laga**
	lah • _ga_
press	**stryka**
	str**ew** • ka
When will it be ready?	**När blir det klart?**
	nair bleer d**ee** klahrt

HAIR & BEAUTY

I'd like…	**Jag vill…**
	yahg vihl…
an appointment for today/ tomorrow	**boka en tid till idag/imorgon**
	b**oa** • ka ehn teed tihl ee • dahg/ ee • mo • ron
some colour/ highlights	**färg/slingor**
	fehry/slihng • ohr
my hair styled/ blow-dried	**få en ny frisyr/föning**
	f**oa** ehn n**ew** free • s**ewr**/funeeng
a hair cut	**få en klippning**
	f**oa** ehn klihp • nihng
an eyebrow/ a bikini wax	**en vaxning av ögonbrynen/bikinilinjen**
	ehn vaks • nihng afv ur • gonn • brew • nehn/ beh • kee • nee • leen • yehn
a facial	**en ansiktsbehandling**
	ehn an • sihkts • beh • hand • lihng
a manicure/ pedicure	**en manikyr/pedikyr**
	ehn ma • nee • kewr/pehd • ee • kewr
a (sports) massage	**(tränings) massage**
	(trair • nihngs •) ma • sahsh
a trim, please…	**en klippning, tack…**
	ehn klihp • nihng, tak

Don't cut it too short.	**Klipp det inte för kort.**
	klihp dee ihn • ter furr koart
Shorter here.	**Kortare här.**
	koar • ta • rer hair
Do you do…?	**Ger ni…?**
	yehr nee…
acupuncture	**akupunktur**
	a • keu • puhnk • teur
aromatherapy	**aroma-terapi**
	a • roa • ma • teh • ra • pee
oxygen treatment	**syrebehandling**
	sew • reh • beh • hand • lihng
Is there a sauna?	**Finns det bastu?**
	fihns dee bas • teu

i

Spas and wellness centers are becoming increasingly popular. There are many to choose from, both in urban and rural areas. It is possible to find spas that offer everything from traditional massage, such as the Swedish massage, which focuses on circulation and relaxation, to yoga, exercise and more. Some are even eco-friendly. Many spas and health centers also have gyms, pools and saunas.

ANTIQUES

How old is this?	**Hur gammalt är det här?**
	heur gam • alt air dee hair
Do you have anything from the … era?	**Har ni något från … perioden?**
	hahr nee noh • gohl frohn … per • eeoh • dehn
Will I have problems with customs?	**Får jag problem i tullen?**
	foar yahg proa • bleem ee tuh • lehn

Is there a certificate of authenticity?	**Finns det ett äkthetsbevis?**
	fihns dee eht ehkt • heets • beh • vees
Can you ship/ wrap it?	**Kan ni skicka/packa in det?**
	kahn nee shih • ka/paka ihn deht

CLOTHING

I'd like…	**Jag skulle vilja ha…**
	yahg skuh • ler vihl • ya hah…
Can I try this on?	**Kan jag prova den här?**
	kan yahg proa • va dehn hair
It doesn't fit.	**Den passar inte.**
	dehn pas • ar ihn • ter
It's too…	**Den är för…**
	dehn air furr…
big	**stor**
	stoar
small	**liten**
	lee • tehn
short	**kort**
	kort
long	**lång**
	loang
tight	**liten**
	leetehn
loose	**stor**
	stohr
Do you have this in size…?	**Har ni den här i storlek…?**
	hahr nee dehn hair ee stoar • leek…
Do you have this in a bigger/smaller size?	**Har ni den här i en större/en mindre storlek?**
	hahr nee dehn hair ee ehn stur • re/ehn mihn • drer stoar • leek

For Numbers, see page 22.

YOU MAY SEE...

HERRKLÄDER	men's clothing
DAMKLÄDER	women's clothing
BARNKLÄDER	children's clothing

YOU MAY HEAR...

Du klär jättebra i den.
Deu klair jai • teh • brah i dehn
That looks great on you.

Hur sitter den?
huhr sih • tehr dehn
How does it fit?

Vi har inte din storlek.
Vee hahr ihnte deen stohr • lehk
We don't have your size.

COLORS

I'm looking for something in...	**Jag söker något i...**
	yahg <u>sur</u> • ker <u>noa</u> • goht ee...
beige	**beige**
	beesh
black	**svart**
	svart
blue	**blått**
	bloat
brown	**brunt**
	br<u>eu</u>nt
gray	**grått**
	groat

green	**grönt**
	grurnt
orange	**orange**
	oa • ransh
pink	**rosa**
	roa • sa
purple	**lila**
	lee • la
red	**rött**
	ruhrt
white	**vitt**
	vit
yellow	**gult**
	geult
I'm looking for something in…	**Jag söker något i…**
	yahg sur • ker noa • goht ee…

CLOTHES & ACCESSORIES

a backpack	**ryggsäck**
	rewg • sehk
a belt	**skärp**
	shairp
a bikini	**bikini**
	bih • kee • nee
a blouse	**blus**
	bleus
a bra	**behå**
	beh • hoa
briefs [underpants]	**kalsonger [underbyxor]**
	khal • sohn • gehr [uhn • dehr • bew • xohr]
panties	**trosor**
	troh·sohr
a coat	**rock**
	rohk

a dress	**klänning**	_klehn_ • ihng
a hat	**hatt**	hat
a jacket	**jacka**	_ya_ • ka
jeans	**jeans**	jeens
pajamas	**pyjamas**	pew • _ya_ • mas
pants [trousers]	**byxor**	_bewx_ • ohr
panty hose [tights]	**strumpbyxor**	_struhmp_ • bewx • ohr
a purse [handbag]	**handväska**	_hand_ • vehs • ka
a raincoat	**regnkappa**	_rehngn_ • kap • a
a scarf	**halsduk**	_hals_ • deuk
a shirt	**skjorta**	_shoar_ • ta
shorts	**shorts**	shohrts
a skirt	**kjol**	choal
socks	**sockar**	_soh_ • kar
stockings	**strumpor**	stuhm • pohr
a suit (jacket and pants)	**kostym**	kos • _tewm_
a suit (jacket and skirt)	**dräkt**	drehkt

sunglasses	**solglasögon**	
	soal • glahs • _**ur**_ • gohn	
a sweater	**tröja**	
	trur • ya	
a sweatshirt	**sweatshirt**	
	sweat • shirt swimming	
swimming trunks	**badbyxor**	
	bahd • bewx • ohr	
a swimsuit	**baddräkt**	
	bahd • drehkt	
a T-shirt	**T-skjorta**	
	tee • shoarta	
a tie	**slips**	
	slihps	
underpants	**kalsonger/trosor**	
(men's/women's)	kal • _soang_ • ehr/_troa_ • sohr	
underwear	**underkläder**	
	uhn • dehr • klai • dehr	

FABRIC

I'd like…	**Jag skulle vilja ha…**	
	yahg _skuh_ • ler _vihl_ • ya hah…	
cotton	**bomull**	
	boam • uhl	
denim	**denim**	
	dehn • ihm	
lace	**spets**	
	spehts	
leather	**läder**	
	lair • der	
linen	**linne**	
	lih • ner	
silk	**siden**	
	see • dehn	

wool	**ull**
	uhl
Is it machine washable?	**Kan det tvättas i maskin?**
	kan dee <u>tveht</u>•as ee ma•<u>sheen</u>

SHOES

I'd like...	**Jag skulle vilja ha...**
	yahg <u>skuh</u>•ler <u>vihl</u>•ya hah...
high-heeled/ flat shoes	**högklackade/lågklackade skor**
	<u>hurg</u>•klak•a•der/<u>loag</u>•klak•a•der skoar
boots	**stövlar**
	<u>stuhv</u>•lar
I'd like...	**Jag skulle vilja ha...**
	yahg <u>skuh</u>•ler <u>vihl</u>•ya hah...
loafers	**loafers**
	<u>loa</u>•fers
sandals	**sandaler**
	san•<u>dahl</u>•ehr
shoes	**skor**
	skoar
slippers	**tofflor**
	<u>toff</u>•lohr
sneakers	**träningsskor**
	<u>trair</u>•nihngs•skoar
In size...	**I storlek...**
	ee <u>stoar</u>•leek...

For Numbers, see page 22.

SIZES

Small (S)	**liten**
	<u>leet</u>•ehn

Medium (M)	**medium**
	mee • dee • uhm
large (L)	**stor**
	st_oar_
extra large (XL)	**extra stor**
	ehx • tra st_oar_
petite	**petite**
	peh • _teet_
plus size	**plus-storlek**
	pleus • st_oar_ • leek

NEWSAGENT & TOBACCONIST

Do you sell English language books/ newspapers?	**Säljer ni böcker/tidningar på engelska?**
	sehl • yehr nee _bur_ • kehr/_teed_ • nihng • ar p_oa_ _ehng_ • ehl • ska
I'd like...	**Jag skulle vilja ha...**
	yahg _skuh_ • ler _vihl_ • ya hah...
candy [sweets]	**godis [sötsaker]**
	g_oa_ • dihs [sut • sahk • ehr]
some chewing gum	**tuggummi**
	tuhg • guh • mee
a chocolate bar	**en chokladkaka**
	ehn shohk • lahd • kahka
some cigars	**några cigarrer**
	noa • gra see • _gahr_ • er
a pack/carton of cigarettes	**ett paket/en limpa cigaretter**
	eht pak • _eht_/ehn _lihm_ • pa sih • ga • _reht_ • her
a lighter	**en tändare**
	ehn _tehn_ • da • rehr
a magazine	**en veckotidning**
	ehn veh • k_oa_ • _teed_ • nihng
matches	**tändstickor**
	tehnd • stik • ohr

a newspaper	**en tidning**
	ehn <u>teed</u> • nihng
a pen	**en penna**
	ehn peh • na
a postcard	**ett vykort**
	eht <u>vew</u> • koart
a road/town map of...	**en vägkarta/stadskarta över...**
	ehn <u>vairg</u> • kahr • ta/<u>stats</u> • kahr • ta <u>ur</u> • vehr...
some stamps	**några frimärken**
	<u>noa</u> • gra <u>free</u> • mair • kehn

PHOTOGRAPHY

I'm looking for... camera.	**Jag skulle vilja köpa...kamera.**
	yahg <u>skuh</u> • ler vihl • ya <u>chur</u> • pa... <u>kah</u> • meh • ra
an automatic	**en automatisk**
	ehn ah • toa • <u>mah</u> • tihsk
a digital	**en digital**
	ehn dih • gih • <u>tahl</u>
a disposable	**en engångs**
	ehn <u>een</u> • goangs
I'd like...	**Jag skulle vilja ha...**
	yahg <u>skuh</u> • ler vihl • ya hah...
a battery	**ett batteri**
	eht ba • teh • <u>ree</u>
a digital print	**ett digitalt kort**
	eht dih • gih • <u>tahlt</u> koart
a memory card	**ett minneskort**
	eht <u>mihn</u> • ehs • koart
Can I print digital photos here?	**Kan jag skriva ut digitala foton här?**
	kan yahg <u>skree</u> • va eut dih • gih • <u>tah</u> • la foh • <u>toan</u> hair

SOUVENIRS

candlesticks	**ljusstakar**
	yeus • stah • kar
Christmas decorations	**juldekorationer**
	yeul • dehk • oh • ra • _shoan_ • ehr
clogs	**träskor**
	trair • skoar
crystal (glass)	**kristallglas**
	kree • _stal_ • glahs
a Dala horse (red wooden horse)	**en dalahäst**
	ehn _dah_ • la • hehst
dolls	**dockor**
	dok • oar
glassware	**glasföremål**
	glahs • furr • reh • m**oa**l
handicrafts	**hemslöjd**
	hehm • sl**uh**yd
horn work	**något i horn**
	_n**oa**_ • goht ee hoarn
jewelry	**smycken**
	_sm**ew**_ • kehn
porcelain	**porslin**
	pohrsh • _leen_
pottery	**keramik**
	cheh • ra • _meek_
reindeer antlers	**renhorn**
	reen • hoarn
Sami handicrafts	**sameslöjd**
	sah • meh • sluhyd
smoked salmon	**rökt lax**
	_rur_kt lax
a tablecloth	**en duk**
	ehn deuk

textiles	**textil**
	tehx • teel
wood carvings	**träfigurer**
	trair • fih • geu • rehr
a wooden knife	**en träkniv**
	ehn trair • kneev
a wooden spoon	**en träsked**
	ehn trair • sheed
Can I see this/that?	**Får jag se på den här/där?**
	foar yahg she poa
	dehn hair/dair
The one in the window/display case.	**Den i fönstret/vitrinet.**
	dehn ee furn • streht/vi • treen • eht
I'd like…	**Jag skulle vilja ha…**
	yahg skuh • ler vihl • ya hah…
a battery	**ett batteri**
	eht ba • teh • ree
a bracelet	**ett armband**
	eht arm • band
a brooch	**en brosch**
	ehn broash
earrings	**örhängen**
	ur • hehng • ehn
a necklace	**ett halsband**
	eht hals • band
a ring	**en ring**
	ehn rihng
a watch	**en armbandsklocka**
	ehn arm • bands • kloh • ka
copper	**koppar**
	kohpp • ar
crystal (quartz)	**kristall**
	krihs • tall

When it comes to souvenirs, whether you are looking for something traditional or modern, you are sure to find just the thing in Sweden. **Träslöjd** (woodwork), **hemslöjd** (handicrafts), **keramik** (ceramics) and Swedish crystal are popular, traditional souvenirs. The **dalahäst** (Dala horse) is perhaps one of the most famous and ubiquitous souvenirs; traditionally, its color is a reddish-orange, but the horses can now be found in a wide range of colors and sizes. Sweden is known for its design, which is evident in its selection of **porslin** (fine china) and ceramics. Some well-known manufacturers include **Höganäs Keramik** and **Rörstrand**, the latter being the second oldest porcelain manufacturer in Europe, founded in 1746. Sweden is also famous for its glass and crystal, both with respect to design and to quality. **Glasriket** (the kingdom of glass) located in Småland, in southeastern Sweden, has around 15 glass factories, including some of the most famous glassworks in Sweden, such as **Kosta Boda**, **Orrefors** and **Nybro**. Factory tours are often available. In addition to the traditional Swedish handicrafts mentioned above, **sameslöjd** (**Sámi** handicraft) is something that should not be overlooked. The **Sámi** are known for their beautiful crafts, which include jewelry and knives carved from reindeer antlers, jewelry made from beaded pewter and reindeer leather as well as a wide range of clothing in reindeer leather and different types of fur.

diamond	**diamant**
	dee • a • mant
white/yellow gold	**vitt/rött guld**
	viht/rurtt geuld

pearl	**pärla**	
	pair • la	
I'd like...	**Jag skulle vilja ha...**	
	yahg <u>skuh</u> • ler <u>vihl</u> • ya hah...	
pewter	**tenn**	
	teen	
platinum	**platina**	
	plah • <u>tee</u> • na	
sterling silver	**äkta silver**	
	<u>ehk</u> • ta <u>sihl</u> • vehr	
Is this real?	**Är den här äkta?**	
	air dehn hair <u>ehk</u> • ta	
Can you engrave it?	**Kan ni gravera den?**	
	kan nee gra • <u>vee</u> • ra dehn	

SPORT & LEISURE

NEED TO KNOW

When's the game?	**När börjar matchen?**	
	nair <u>bur</u> • yar ma • shchehn	
Where's...?	**Var ligger...?**	
	vahr <u>lih</u> • gehr...	
the beach	**stranden**	
	<u>stran</u> • dehn	
Where's...?	**Var ligger...?**	
	vahr <u>lih</u> • gehr...	
the park	**parken**	
	<u>park</u> • ehn	
the pool	**simbassängen**	
	<u>sihm</u> • ba • sehng • ehn	

Is it safe to swim/ dive here?	**Kan man simma/dyka här utan risk?**
	kan man sihmm•a/dew•ka hair eu•tan rihsk
Can I rent [hire] golf clubs?	**Kan man hyra golfklubbor?**
	kan man hew•ra gohlf•kluh•bohr
How much per hour?	**Vad kostar det per timme?**
	vahd kos•tar dee pair tihm•er
How far is it to...?	**Hur långt är det till...?**
	heur loangt air dee tihl...
Can you show me on the map?	**Kan du visa mig på kartan?**
	kan deu vee sa may poa kahr•tan

WATCHING SPORT

When's...?	**När börjar...?**
	nair bur•yar...
the baseball game	**basebollmatchen**
	base•bohl•mat•shehn
the basketball game	**basketbollmatchen**
	bahs•keht•bohl•ma•shchehn

Sports and recreation are popular, and there are excellent sports facilities everywhere, ranging from **golf** (golf), **fiske** (fishing), **tennis** (tennis) and **fotboll** (soccer) to **skidåkning** (skiing) and **ishockey** (ice hockey). Tourist offices should have contact information for the various sports facilities in your area. Swedes also love the great outdoors, and the country has much to offer when it comes to **bergklättring** (mountain climbing), **vandring** (hiking), **ridsport** (horsebackriding), **cykelåkning** (cycling), **paddla kanot** (canoeing) and **segling** (boating). Whether you are looking for a day hike or planning a longer trip, some great choices include **Kebnekaise**, which is Sweden's highest mountain, **Kungsleden**, **Bohusleden** or **Padjelantleden**. There are a lot of options for cyclists, both amateurs and professionals, and popular cycle routes include **Kustlinjen** and **Sverigeleden**.

the boxing match	**boxningsmatchen**
	boax • nihngs • matsh • ehn
the cricket game	**cricketspelet**
	cricket • matsh • ehn
the cycling race	**cykeltävlingen**
	sew • kehl • taiv • lihng • ehn
the golf tournament	**golfspelet**
	golf • spee • leht
the soccer [football] game	**fotbollsmatchen**
	foat • bohls • ma • shchehn
the tennis match	**tennismatchen**
	tehn • ihs • ma • shchehn
the volleyball game	**volleybollspelet**
	voh • lee • bohl • spee • leht

Which teams are playing?	**Vilka lag spelar?**
	vihl • ka lahg _spee_ • lar
Where's the stadium?	**Var ligger idrottsarenan?**
	vahr _lih_ • gehr _ee_ • drohts • a • _ree_ • nan
Where's the horsetrack/racetrack?	**Var finns hästkapplöpnings/kapplöpningsbanan?**
	Vahr fihns hehst • _kap_ • luhp • nihngs/kahp • luhp • nihgs • bahn • an
Where can I place a bet?	**Var kan jag spela lotto?**
	vahr kan yahg _spee_ • la _loh_ • toa

PLAYING SPORT

Is there…nearby?	**Finns det…i närheten?**
	fihns d**ee**…ee _nair_ • hee • ten
a golf course	**en golfbana**
	ehn _gohlf_ • bah • na
a gym	**ett gym**
	eht yim
a park	**en park**
	ehn park
a tennis court	**en tennisbana**
	ehn _tehn_ • ihs • bah • nohr
How much per…?	**Hur mycket kostar det per…?**
	heur _mew_ • ker _kos_ • tar d**ee** pair…
day	**dag**
	dahg
hour	**timme**
	tihm • er
game	**spel**
	speel
round	**runda**
	ruhn • da
Can I rent [hire]…?	**Kan man hyra…?**
	kan man _hew_ • ra…

golf clubs	**klubbor**
	kluhb • ohr
equipment	**utrustning**
	eut • ruhst • nihng
a racket	**en racket**
	ehn ra • keht

AT THE BEACH/POOL

Where's the beach/ pool?	**Var är stranden/simbassängen?**
	vahr air stran • dehn/ sihm • ba • sehng • ehn
Is there a…here?	**Finns det…här?**
	fihns dee…hair
a kiddie [paddling] pool	**en barnbassäng**
	ehn bahrn • bah • sehng
an indoor/ outdoor pool	**en inomhuspool/utomhuspool**
	ehn in • ohm • heus • poal/ eut • ohm • heus • poal
a lifeguard	**en livräddare**
	leev • rehd • a • rer
Is it safe to swim/ dive?	**Kan man simma/dyka här utan risk?**
	Kan man sihm • a/dew • ka hair eu • tan rihsk
Is it safe for children?	**Är det barnsäkert?**
	air dee bahrn • sair • kert
I want to hire…	**Jag skulle vilja hyra…**
	yahg skuh • ker vihl • ya hew • ra…
a deck chair	**en solstol**
	ehn soal • stoal
diving equipment	**dykutrustning**
	dewk • uht • ruhst • nihng
a jet ski	**en jetski**
	ehn jeht • skee

a motorboat	**en motorbåt**
	ehn moa • tor • boat
a rowboat	**en roddbåt**
	ehn rohd • boat
snorkeling equipment	**snorklingsutrustning**
	snoh • rklihngs • uht • ruhst • nihng
a surfboard	**en surfbräda**
	ehn suhrf • brair • da
a towel	**en handduk**
	ehn hand • deuk
an umbrella	**en solparasol**
	ehn soal • pa • ra • sohl
water skis	**vattenskidor**
	va • tehrn • shee • dohr
a windsurfer	**en vindsurfare**
	ehn vihnd • suhr • fa • reh

For Traveling with Children, see page 134.

A significant portion of the Swedish coastline is rough, covered with granite rocks and cliffs and dotted with beaches. Most of the sandy beaches are found in the south and on the southwest coasts. Around Stockholm you can swim and dive from the small islands in the archipelago — and you can even swim in the water around Stockholm itself. Inland lakes, coastal areas and the popular archipelagos of Stockholm and the West Coast are perfect for boaters, canoeists and kayakers alike.

WINTER SPORTS

A lift pass for a day/ five days, please.	**Ett liftpass för en dag/för fem dagar, tack.** *eht lihft • pas furr ehn dahg/furr fehm dahg • ar tak*
Where's the ice rink?	**Var ligger isbanan?** *vahr lee • gehr ihs • bahn • an*
Are there lessons?	**Kan man få lektioner?** *kan man foa lehk • shoa • nehr*
How much?	**Hur mycket?** *huhr mew • keh*
I'm a beginner.	**Jag är nybörjare.** *yahg air new • bur • yah • reh*
I'm experienced.	**Jag har erfarenhet.** *yahg hahr air • fah • rehn • heet*

Swedes grow up with skiing: cross-country in the south and downhill in the north. There are many excellent ski resorts in the north, offering superb skiing and first-class facilities. Many hotels offer three- to seven-day package deals, including transportation and accommodation. In June, try **Riksgränsen** for a taste of skiing in the midnight sun.

Långfärdsbussar (long-distance buses) are efficient, relatively cheap and run daily to all major towns and resorts. Most of the major ski resorts also offer other winter sport activities like snowmobile safaris, snowshoeing and dog sledding tours. **Ishotellet** (Ice Hotel), though not a ski resort specifically, does offer several of these activities.

I'd like to hire...	**Jag skulle vilja hyra...**
	yahg skuh•ler vihl•ya hew•ra...
boots	**skidpjäxor**
	sheed•pyeaix•ohr
a helmet	**en hjälm**
	ehn yehlm
ice skates	**skridskor**
	skrih•skohr
poles	**stavar**
	stah•var
skis	**skidor**
	shee•dohr
a snowboard	**en snowboard**
	ehn snow•board
snowshoes	**pjäxor**
	pyaix•ohr
These are too big/small.	**De här är för stora/små.**
	dehm hair air furr stoa•ra/smoa
A trail [piste] map, please.	**En karta över spåren, tack.**
	ehn kahr•ta ur•vehr spoa•rehn tak

YOU MAY SEE...

DRAGLIFT	drag lift
ÄGGLIFT	cable car
STOLLIFT	chair lift
NYBÖRJARE	novice
MELLANNIVÅ	intermediate
AVANCERAD	expert
SPÅRET STÄNGD	trail [piste] closed

OUT IN THE COUNTRY

I'd like a map of…	**Jag skulle vilja ha en karta över…**
	yahg <u>skuh</u> • ler <u>vihl</u> • ya hah ehn <u>kahr</u> • ta <u>ur</u> • vehr…
this region	**denna region**
	<u>dehn</u> • a reh • <u>gioan</u>
walking routes	**vandringsleder**
	<u>van</u> • drihngs • <u>lee</u> • dehr
cycle routes	**cykeleder**
	<u>sew</u> • kehl • <u>lee</u> • dehr
the trails	**spåren**
	<u>spoa</u> • rehn
Is it easy/difficult?	**Är det lätt/svårt?**
	air dee leht/svoart
Is it far/steep?	**Är det långt/brant?**
	air dee loangt/brant
How far is it to…?	**Hur långt är det till…?**
	heur <u>loangt</u> air dee tihl…
Can you show me on the map?	**Kan du visa mig på kartan?**
	kan deu <u>vee</u> • sa may poa <u>kahr</u> • tan
I'm lost.	**Jag har kommit vilse.**
	yahg hahr <u>koh</u> • miht <u>vihl</u> • ser

Where's…?	**Var ligger…?**
	vahr lih • gehr…
the bridge	**bron**
	broan
the cave	**grottan**
	groht • an
the cliff	**klippa**
	klihp • an
the farm	**bondgården**
	boand • goard • ehn
the field	**åkern**
	oak • ern
the footpath	**fotvandringsleden**
	foat • vand • rihngs • lee • dehn
the forest	**skogen**
	skoag • ehn
the hill	**berget**
	behr • yeht
the lake	**sjön**
	shurn
the mountain	**berget**
	behr • yeht
the mountain pass	**bergspasset**
	berys • pas • eht
the mountain range	**bergskedjan**
	berys • chee • dyan
the nature reserve	**naturreservatet**
	na • teur • res • her • vah • teht
the panorama	**panoraman**
	pan • o • rah • man
the park	**parken**
	park • ehn
the path	**stigen**
	stee • gehn

Where's...?	**Var ligger...?**
	vahr <u>lih</u> • gehr...
the peak	**toppen**
	<u>tohp</u> • ehn
the picnic area/	**picknickområdet/rastplatsen**
rest area	*pihk • nihk • ohm • <u>roa</u> • det/<u>rast</u> • plats • ehn*
the pond	**dammen**
	dah • mehn
the river	**floden**
	fl<u>oad</u> • ehn
the sea	**havet**
	<u>hafv</u> • eht
the hot spring	**den varma källan**
	dehn var • ma cheh • lan
the valley	**dalen**
	<u>dahl</u> • ehn
the viewpoint	**utsiktspunkten**
	<u>eut</u> • sihkts • peunk • tehn
the village	**byn**
	bewn
the vineyard	**vinodlingen**
	vihn • ohd • lihng • ehn
the waterfall	**vattenfallet**
	<u>va</u> • tehrn • fal

TRAVELING WITH CHILDREN

NEED TO KNOW

Is there a discount for kids?	**Har ni barnrabatt?**
	hahr nee bahrn • rah • bat
Can you recommend a babysitter?	**Kan du rekommendera en barnvakt?**
	kan deu reh • koh • mehn • dee • ra ehn bahrn • vakt
Could I have a highchair?	**Kan jag få en barnstol, tack?**
	kan yahg foa ehn bahrn • stoal tak
Where can I change the baby?	**Var kan jag byta på babyn?**
	vahr kan yahg bew • ta poa bai • been
Where's...?	**Var ligger...?**
	vahr lih • gehr...
the amusement park	**nöjesfältet**
	nury • ehs • fehl • teht
the arcade	**arkadhallen**
	ar • kahd • ha • lehn
the kiddie [paddling] pool	**barnbassängen**
	bahrn • ba • sehng • ehn
the park	**parken**
	park • kehn
the playground	**lekplatsen**
	leek • plats • ehn
the zoo	**djurparken**
	yeur • park • ehn
Are kids allowed?	**Får man ta barnen med?**
	foar man tah bahr • nehn meed
Is it safe for kids?	**Är det barnsäkert?**
	air det bahrn • sair • kert

YOU MAY HEAR...

Vad gullig!
vahd <u>geul</u> • ig

How cute!

Vad heter han/hon?
vahd <u>hee</u> • tehr han/hoan

What's his/her name?

Hur gammal är han/hon?
heur <u>gam</u> • al air han/hoan

How old is he/she?

OUT & ABOUT

Can you recommend something for kids?	**Kan du föreslå något för barn?** *kan deu <u>furr</u> • reh • s<u>loa noa</u> • goht furr bahrn*
Where's...?	**Var är...?** *Vahr air...*
the amusement park	**nöjesparken** *nuy • ehs • pahr • kehn*
the arcade	**gallerian** *gah • le • ree • an*
the kiddie [paddling] pool	**barnbassängen/plaskdammen** *bah • rn • ba • sehng • ehn/ plask • da • mehn*
the park	**parken** *par • kehn*
the playground	**lekplatsen** *lehk • plat • sehn*
the zoo	**djurparken** *yeur • par • kehn*
Are kids allowed?	**Tillåts barn?** *tihl • oats bahrn*
Is it safe for kids?	**Är det säkert för barn?** *air deht seh • kehrt furr bahrn*

| Is it suitable for… year olds? | **Passar det för…-åringar?** |
| | _pas_ • ar dee furr…_oa_ • rihng • ar |

For Numbers, see page 22.

BABY ESSENTIALS

Do you have…?	**Har ni…?**
	hahr nee…
a baby bottle	**en nappflaska**
	ehn nap • flas • ka
baby food	**babymat**
	behy • bih • maht
baby wipes	**våtservetter för barn**
	voat • ser • veht • er furrbahrn
a car seat	**en bilbarnstol**
	ehn beel • bahrn • stoal
a children's menu	**en barnmeny**
	ehn bahrn • meh • new
a children's portion	**en barnportion**
	bahrn • pohrt • shoan
a highchair	**en barnstol**
	ehn bahrn • stoal

a crib	**en barnsäng**
	ehn bahrn • sehng
diapers [nappies]	**blöjor**
	blury • ohr
formula	**välling**
	vehl • ihng
a pacifier [dummy]	**en napp**
	ehn nap
a playpen	**ett lekrum**
	eht leek • ruhm
a stroller	**en sittvagn**
[pushchair]	*ehn siht • vangn*
Can I breastfeed the baby here?	**Får jag amma barnet här?**
	foar yahg ah • ma bahr • neht hair
Where can I change the baby?	**Var kan jag byta på babyn?**
	vahr kan yahg bew • ta poa bai • been

For Dining with Children, see page 168.

BABYSITTING

Can you recommend a reliable babysitter?	**Kan du rekommendera en pålitlig barnvakt?**
	kaun deu re • koh • mehn • dee • rahra ehn poa • leet • lihg bahrn • vakt
What's the charge?	**Vad kostar det?**
	vahd kos • tar dee
We'll be back by...	**Vi kommer tillbaka**
	Vee koh • mehr tihl • bah • ka
I'll pick them up at...	**Jag hämtar dem...**
	yahg hehm • tar dehm...
I can be reached at...	**Du kan nå mig på...**
	deu kan noa may poa...

For Time, see page 24

SAFE TRAVEL

EMERGENCIES

NEED TO KNOW

Help!	**Hjälp!**
	yelp
Go away!	**Ge er iväg!**
	yeh ehr ee • vairg
Stop thief!	**Stoppa tjuven!**
	stop • a shcheu • vehn
Get a doctor!	**Hämta en läkare!**
	hehm • ta ehn lair • ka • rer
Fire!	**Det brinner!**
	dee brihn • ehr
I'm lost.	**Jag har gått vilse.**
	yahg hahr goat vihl • ser
Can you help me?	**Kan du hjälpa mig?**
	kan deu yehl • pa may

YOU MAY HEAR...

Fyll i blanketten, tack.
fewl ee blan • keht • ehn tak
Please fill out this form.

Er legitimation, tack.
ehr lehg • ee • tih • ma • shoan tak
Your identification, please.

När/Var hände det?
nair/vahr hehn • dehr dee
When/Where did it happen?

Hur ser han/hon ut?
hewr seer han/hoan eut
What does he/she look like?

POLICE

In an emergency, dial: **112**.
This number will connect you to the police, the fire
brigade or an ambulance.

NEED TO KNOW

Call the police!	**Ring polisen!**
	rihng poa • lee • sehn
Where's the nearest police station?	**Var ligger närmaste polisstation?**
	vahr lih • gehr nair • mas • ter poo • lees • sta • shoan
There's been an accident.	**Det har hänt en olycka.**
	det hahr hehnt ehn oa • lewk • a
I've been attacked.	**Jag har blivit anfallen.**
	jahg hahr blee • viht an • fa • lehn
My child is missing.	**Mitt barn har kommit bort.**
	miht bahrn hahr koh • miht bohrt
I need…	**Jag behöver…**
	yahg beh • hur • vehr…
an interpreter	**en tolk**
	ehn tohlk
to contact my lawyer	**kontakta min advokat**
	kohn • tak • ta mihn ad • voh • kaht
to make a phone call	**ringa ett samtal**
	rihng • a eht sam • tahl
I'm innocent.	**Jag är oskyldig.**
	yahg air oa • shewl • dihg

CRIME & LOST PROPERTY

I want to report...	**Jag vill anmäla...**
	yahg vihl <u>an</u> • mair • la...
a mugging	**ett överfall**
	eht <u>ur</u> • vehr • fal
a rape	**en våldtäkt**
	ehn <u>vohld</u> • tehkt
a theft	**ett rån**
	eht roan
I've been robbed/ mugged.	**Jag har blivit rånad/överfallen.**
	yahg hahr <u>blee</u> • viht <u>roa</u> • nad/ <u>ur</u> • veh • fal • ehn
I've lost...	**Jag har tappet...**
	yahg hahr <u>tah</u> • pat...
My...has been stolen.	**Någon har stulit...**
	<u>noa</u> • gohn hahr <u>steu</u> • liht...
backpack	**min ryggsäck**
	mihn <u>rewg</u> • sehk
bicycle	**min cykel**
	mihn <u>sew</u> • kehl
camera	**min kamera**
	mihn <u>kah</u> • meh • ra

rental car	**min bil/hyrbil**
	mihn beel/<u>hewr</u> • beel
computer	**min dator**
	mihn <u>dah</u> • tohr
credit cards	**mina kreditkort**
	mee • na kre • <u>deet</u> • koart
jewelry	**mina smycken**
	mee • na <u>smew</u> • ken
money	**mina pengar**
	mee • na <u>pehng</u> • ar
passport	**mitt pass**
	miht pas
purse [handbag]	**min portmonnä**
	mihn pohrt • mo • <u>nai</u>
traveler's checks	**mina resecheckar**
[cheques]	*<u>mee</u> • na <u>ree</u> • seh • shehk • ar*
wallet	**min plånbok**
	mihn <u>ploan</u> • boak
I need a police report for my insurance.	**Jag behöver en polisanmälan till min försäkring.**
	yahg beh • hu • vehr ehn poal • ees • an • mailan tihl meen furr • sehk·rihng
Where is the British/ American/Irish embassy?	**Var ligger den brittiska/amerikanska ambassaden?**
	var ligger den brittiska/amerikanska ambassaden?

HEALTH

NEED TO KNOW

I'm sick [ill].	**Jag är sjuk.**
	yahg air sheuk
I need an English-speaking doctor.	**Jag behöver en engelsktalande läkare.**
	yahg beh • hur • vehr ehn
	ehng • ehlsk • tahl • an • der
	lair • ka • rer
It hurts here.	**Det gör ont här.**
	dee yurr oant hair
I have a stomachache.	**Jag har ont i magen.**
	yahg hahr oant ee mah • gehn

FINDING A DOCTOR

Can you recommend a doctor/dentist?	**Kan du rekommendera en läkare/tandläkare?**
	kan deu reh • koh • mehn • dee • ra ehn
	lair • ka • rer/tand • lair • ka • rer
Can the doctor come to see me here?	**Kan doktorn komma och undersöka mig här?**
	kan dohk • torn koh • ma ohk
	eun • der • sur • ka may hair
I need an English-speaking doctor.	**Jag behöver en engelsktalande läkare.**
	yahg beh • uv • ehr en
	eeng • ehlsk • tah • lan • de leh • ka • re
What are their office hours?	**Vilka är deras öppettider?**
	vihl • ka air dee • ras ur • peh • tee • dehr

Can I make an appointment for...?	**Kan jag boka en tid...?**
	kan yahg boa • ka ehn teed...
today	**idag**
	ee • dahg
tomorrow	**imorgon**
	ee • mo • ron
as soon as possible	**så snart som möjligt**
	soa snahrt som mury • ligt
It's urgent.	**Det är brådskande.**
	dee air broas • kan • der

SYMPTOMS

I'm...	**Jag...**
	yahg...
bleeding	**blöder**
	blur • dehr
constipated	**är förstoppad**
	air furr • stop • ad
dizzy	**har yrsel**
	hahr ewr • sehl
nauseous	**mår illa**
	moar ihl • la

vomiting	**kräks**
	krairks
It hurts here.	**Det gör ont här.**
	dee yurr oant hair
I have…	**Jag har…**
	yahg hahr…
an allergic reaction	**en allergisk reaktion**
	ehn a•lehr•<u>gihsk</u> ree•ak•<u>shoan</u>
chest pain	**ont i bröstet**
	oant ee <u>brurs</u>•teht
cramps	**kramper**
	kram•pehr
diarrhea	**diarré**
	dee•ar•ee
an earache	**ont i örat**
	oant ee <u>ur</u>•rat
a fever	**feber**
	<u>fee</u>•behr
pain	**ont**
	oant
a rash	**ett utslag**
	eht <u>eut</u>•slahg
a sprain	**en stukning**
	ehn <u>steuk</u>•nihng
some swelling	**en lätt svullnad**
	ehn leht <u>sveul</u>•nad
a stomachache	**ont i magen**
	oant ee <u>mah</u>•gehn
sunstroke	**solsting**
	<u>soal</u>•stihng
I've been sick [ill] for…days.	**Jag har varit sjuk i…dagar.**
	yahg hahr <u>vah</u>•riht sheuk ee…<u>dah</u>•gar

For Numbers, see page 22.

YOU MAY HEAR...

Vad är det för fel?
vahd air dee fur feel

Var gör det ont?
vahr yur dee oant

Gör det ont här?
yur deht ohnt hehr

Tar du någon annan medicin?
*tahr deu <u>noa</u> • gohn <u>an</u> • an
meh • dih • seen*

Är du allergisk mot något?
air deu a • lehr • <u>gihsk</u> moat <u>noa</u> • goht

Öppna munnen.
<u>urp</u> • na <u>muhn</u> • ehn

Andas djupt.
<u>an</u> • das yeupt

Hosta, tack.
hoas • ta, tak

Du behöver åka till sjukhuset.
*deu beh • <u>hur</u> • vehr oa • ka tihl
<u>sjeuk</u> • <u>heu</u> • seht*

What's wrong?
Where does it hurt?
Does it hurt here?
Are you taking any other medication?
Are you allergic to anything?
Open your mouth.
Breathe deeply.
Cough, please.

You need to go to the hospital.

CONDITIONS

I'm anemic/diabetic.
Jag är anemisk/diabetiker.
*yahg air a • <u>nee</u> • mihsk/
dee • a • <u>beh</u> • tih • ker*

I'm epileptic.
Jag har epilepsi.
yahg hahr eh • pih • leh • psi

I'm allergic to antibiotics/ penicillin.	**Jag är allergisk mot antibiotika/ penicillin.**
	yahg air a • lehr • gihsk moat an • tih • bee • oa • tee • ka/ pehn • eh • si • leen
I have...	**Jag har...**
	yahg hahr...
arthritis	**artrit**
	ar • treet
asthma	**astma**
	as • ma
high/low blood pressure	**högt/låg blodtryck**
	hurgt/loagt bload • trewk
a heart condition	**hjärtproblem**
	yairt • proa • bleem
I'm taking... (medicine).	**Jag tar...(medicin).**
	yahg tahr...(meh • dee • seen)

TREATMENT

Can you prescribe a generic drug [unbranded medication]?	**Kan du skriva ut ett generiskt läkemedel [generika]?**
	Kahn deu skrih • va eut eht gehn • eh • rih • skt lai • keh • meh • dehl [gehn • eh • rih • ka]
Where can I get it?	**Var hittar jag det?**
	vahr hih • tar yahg deht
Do I need a prescription/ medicine?	**Behöver jag ett recept/medicin?**
	beh • hur • vehr yahg eht reh • sehpt/ meh • dih • sihn

For Pharmacy, see page 151.

HOSPITAL

Please notify my family.	**Var snäll och underrätta min familj.**
	vahr snehl ohk <u>eun</u> • der • rehta mihn <u>fa</u> • mily
I'm in pain.	**Jag har ont.**
	yahg hahr oant
I need a doctor/nurse.	**Jag behöver en läkare/sjuksköterska.**
	yahg beh • <u>hur</u> • vehr ehn <u>lair</u> • ka • rer/ sheuk • <u>shur</u> • ter • ska
When are visiting hours?	**När är det besökstid?**
	nair air d<u>ee</u> beh • <u>surks</u> • teed
I'm visiting…	**Jag vill besöka…**
	yahg vihl beh • <u>sur</u> • ka…

DENTIST

I've broken a tooth/lost a filling.	**Jag har brutit av en tand/tappat en plomb.**
	yahg hahr <u>breu</u> • tiht afv ehn tand/<u>tap</u> • at ehn plohmb
This tooth hurts.	**Den här tanden gör ont.**
	dehn hair <u>tan</u> • dehn y<u>ur</u> oant
Can you fix this denture?	**Kan du reparera den här tandprotesen?**
	kan deu reh • <u>pa</u> • <u>ree</u> • ra dehn hair <u>tand</u> • proh • <u>tees</u> • ehn

GYNECOLOGIST

I have menstrual cramps/a vaginal infection.	**Jag har mens värk/en vaginal infektion.**
	yahg hahr mens vehrk/ehn va • gih • <u>nahl</u> ihn • fehk • <u>shoan</u>
I missed my period.	**Min mens har inte kommit.**
	mihn mehns hahr <u>ihn</u> • ter <u>koh</u> • miht

I'm on the Pill.	**Jag tar p-piller.**
	yahg tahr pee • pihl • ler
I'm (…months) pregnant.	**Jag är (…månader) gravid.**
	Yahg air (…moh • na • dehr) gra • veed
I'm (not) pregnant.	**Jag är (inte) gravid.**
	yahg air (ihn • ter) gra • veed
I haven't had my period for…months.	**Jag har inte haft mens på… månader.**
	yahg hahr ihn • ter haft mehns poa… moa • na • dehr

For Numbers, see page 22.

OPTICIAN

I've lost…	**Jag har tappat…**
	yahg hahr tap • at…
a contact lens	**en kontaktlins**
	ehn kohn • takt • lihns
my glasses	**mina glasögon**
	mee • na glahs • ur • gohn
a lens	**en lins**
	ehn lihns

PAYMENT & INSURANCE

How much does it cost?	**Hur mycket kostar det?**
	heur mew • ker kos • tar dee
Can I pay by credit card?	**Kan jag betala med kreditkort?**
	kan yahg beh • tah • la meed kreh • deet • koart
I have insurance.	**Jag har försäkring.**
	yahg hahr furr • sair • krihng

Can I have a receipt for my insurance?
Kan jag få ett kvitto för mitt försäkringsbolag?
kan yahg foa eht kvih • toh furr miht furr • sair • krihngs • boa • lahg

PHARMACY

NEED TO KNOW

Where's the nearest pharmacy?
Var är närmaste apotek?
vahr air nair • mas • teh a • poa • teek

What time does the pharmacy open/close?
När öppnar/stänger apoteket?
nair urp • nar/ stehng • ehr a • poa • tee • keht

What would you recommend for...?
Vad kan du rekommendera för...?
vahd kan deu reh • koh • mehn • dee • ra furr...

How much should I take?
Hur mycket ska jag ta?
heur mew • ker skah yahg tah

Can you fill [make up] this prescription for me?
Kan ni göra iordning det här receptet åt mig?
kan nee yur • ra ee oard • nihng dee hair reh • sehp • teht oat may

I'm allergic to...
Jag är allergisk mot...
yahg air a • lehr • gihsk moat...

WHAT TO TAKE

How much should I take?
Hur mycket ska jag ta?
heur mew • ker skah yahg tah

How many times a day should I take it?	**Hur många gånger om dagen ska jag ta det?**
	heur moang • a goang • er ohm dah • gehn skah yahg tah dee
Is it suitable for children?	**Är det lämpligt för barn?**
	air dee lehmp • lihgt furr bahrn
I'm taking… (medicine).	**Jag tar…(medicin).**
	yahg tahr…(meh • dee • seen)
Are there side effects?	**Ger det några biverkningar?**
	yehr dee noa • gra bee • vehrk • nihng • ar
I'd like some medicine for…	**Jag behöver medicin mot…**
	yahg beh • hur • vehr meh • dih • seen moat…

a cold	**en förkylning**
	ehn furr • chewl • nihng
a cough	**hosta**
	hoas • ta
diarrhea	**diarré**
	dee • a • reh
a headache	**huvudvärk**
	huh • vuhd • vairk
an insect bite	**ett insektbett**
	eht in • sekt • beht
motion sickness	**åksjuka**
	oak • sheu • ka
a sore throat	**halsont**
	hals • oant
a sunburn	**solbränna**
	soal • brehn • a
a toothache	**tandvärk**
	tand • vairk
an upset stomach	**ont i magen**
	oant ee mah • gehn

In addition to filling prescriptions, **apotek** (pharmacies) sell over-the-counter medication as well as their own brands of toiletries and cosmetics. Almost all pharmacies are open on weekdays, but not all are open late in the evening or on weekends. Business hours vary considerably depending on the pharmacy. Generally, business hours are between 9:00 a.m. and 5:00 p.m. on weekdays. Pharmacies that are open in the evening usually close around 9:00 p.m., and weekend hours are generally from 10:00 a.m. to 4:00 p.m.

YOU MAY SEE...

EN GÅNG/TRE GÅNGER PER DAG	once/three times a day
TABLETTER	tablets
DROPPAR TESKEDAR	drop teaspoons
FÖRE/EFTER/TILLSAMMANS MED MÅLTIDER	before/after/ with meals
PÅ FASTANDE MAGE	on an empty stomach
SVÄLJS HELA	swallow whole
KAN ORSAKA DÅSIGHET	may cause drowsiness
ENDAST FÖR UTVÄRTES BRUK	for external use only

BASIC SUPPLIES

I'd like...	**Jag skulle vilja ha...**
	yahg skuh•ler vihl•ya hah...
acetaminophen [paracetamol]	**acetominofen**
	a•seht•a•mihn•oa•fehn
antiseptic cream	**antiseptisk salva**
	an•tih•sehp•tihsk sal•va
aspirin	**huvudvärkstabletter**
	heu•vuhd•vairks•ta•bleh•ter
bandage [plasters]	**gasbinda**
	gahs•bihn•da
a comb	**kam**
	kam
condoms	**kondomer**
	kohn•doa•mehr
contact lens solution	**kontaktlinsvätska**
	kohn•takt•lins•veht•ska
deodorant	**deodorant**
	dee•oa•deh•rant
a hairbrush	**en hårborste**
	ehn hoar•bohrsh•ter
hair spray	**hårspray**
	hoar•spray
ibuprofen	**ibuprofen**
	ee•beu•proa•fehn
insect repellent	**myggolja**
	mewg•ohl•ya
a nail file	**en nagelfil**
	ehn nah•gehl•feel
a (disposable) razor	**en (engångs)-rakhyvel**
	ehn (een•goangs)•rahk•hew•vehl
razor blades	**rakblad**
	rahk•blahd

sanitary napkins [towels]	**bindor**
	bin • dohr
shampoo/	**schampo**
	sham • poa
conditioner	**hårbalsam**
	hoar • bal • sam
soap	**tvål**
	tv_oal_
sunscreen	**solskyddskräm**
	soal • shewds • krairm
tampons	**tamponger**
	tam • _poang_ • ehr
tissue	**papper näsdukar**
	_pa_ • pehrs • nairs • _deu_ • kar
toilet paper	**toalettpapper**
	toa • a • _leht_ • pa • pehr
a toothbrush	**tandborste**
	tand • bohr • ster
toothpaste	**tandkräm**
	tand • krairm

For Baby Essentials, see page 136.

CHILD HEALTH & EMERGENCY

Can you recommend a pediatrician?	**Kan du rekommendera en barnläkare?**
	kan deu reh • koh • men • _dee_ • ra ehn bahrn • _lairk_ • a • rer
My child is allergic to…	**Mitt barn är allergiskt mot…**
	miht bahrn air a • _lehr_ • gisk m_oat_…
My child is missing.	**Mitt barn har kommit bort.**
	miht bahrn hahr _koh_ • miht bohrt
Have you seen a boy/girl?	**Har du sett en pojke/flicka?**
	hahr deu seht ehn _poy_ • ker/_flih_ • ka

DISABLED TRAVELERS

NEED TO KNOW

Is there...?	**Finns det...?** *fihns det...*
access for the disabled	**ingång för rörelsehindrade** *in • goang furr* *rur • rehl • seh • hihn • dra • der*
a wheelchair ramp	**en rullstolsramp** *ehn reul • stoals • ramp*
a disabled-accessible toilet	**en handikappanpassad toalett** *ehn hand • ee • kap • an • pas • ad* *toa • ah • leht*
I need...	**Jag behöver...** *yahg beh • hur • ver...*
assistance	**hjälp** *yehlp*
an elevator [lift]	**en hiss** *ehn hihs*
a ground floor room	**ett rum på bottenvåningen** *eht ruhm poa* *boh • tehrn • voa • nihng • hen*

ASKING FOR ASSISTANCE

I'm disabled.	**Jag är handikappad.** *yahg air hand • ee • kap • ad*
I'm deaf.	**Jag är döv.** *yahg air durv*

I'm visually/hearing impaired.	**Jag är synskadad/hörselskadad.**
	yahg air <u>sewn</u> • skah • dad/ hur • sel • <u>skah</u> • dad
I'm unable to walk far/use the stairs.	**Jag kan inte gå långt/gå i trappor.**
	yahg kan <u>ihn</u> • ter goa loangt/goa ee <u>trap</u> • ohr
Can I bring my wheelchair?	**Kan jag ta med min rullstol?**
	kan yahg tah meed mihn ruhl • stoal
Are guide dogs permitted?	**Är det tillåtet med ledarhund?**
	air dee tihl • <u>loa</u> • teht meed <u>leed</u> • ar • huhnd
Can you help me?	**Kan du hjälpa mig?**
	kan deu yehl • pa may
Could you open/hold the door?	**Kan du öppna/hålla upp dörren?**
	kan deu <u>urp</u> • na/<u>hoa</u> • la uhp <u>dur</u> • rehn

For Health, see page 144.

FOOD

EATING OUT

NEED TO KNOW

Can you recommend a good restaurant/ bar?	**Kan du rekommendera en bra restaurang/pub?** *kan deu reh • koh • mehn • dee • ra ehn brah rehs • teu • rang/peub*
Is there a traditional Swedish/an inexpensive restaurant nearby?	**Finns det något värdshus/någon billigare restaurang i närheten?** *fihns dee noa • goht vairds • heus/ noa • gohn bihl • ih • ga • rer rehs • teu • rang ee nair • hee • tehn*
A table for..., please.	**Ett bord för..., tack.** *eht bohrd furr...tak*
Could we sit...?	**Får vi sitta...?** *foar vee siht • a...*
here/there	**här/där** *hair/dair*
outside	**ute** *eu • ter*

in a non-smoking area	**vid bord för icke-rökare** *veed bohrd furr ee • keh • rur • ka • rer*
I'm waiting for someone.	**Jag väntar på någon.** *yahg vairn • tar poa noa • gohn*
Where are the toilets?	**Var finns toaletten?** *vahr fihns toa • ah • leh • tehn*
A menu, please.	**En meny, tack.** *ehn meh • neu tak*
What do you recommend?	**Vad rekommenderar du?** *vahd reh • koh • mehn • dee • rar deu*
I'd like…	**Jag skulle vilja ha…** *yahg skuh • ler vihl • ya hah…*
Some more…, please.	**Lite mer…, tack.** *lee • ter meer…tak*
Enjoy your meal.	**Smaklig måltid.** *smahk • lihg moal • teed*
The check [bill], please.	**Kan jag få räkningen, tack.** *kan yahg foa rairk • nihng • ehn tak*
Is service included?	**Är serveringsavgiften inräknad?** *air ser • veeh • rihngs • afv • yihf • tehn ihn • rairk • nad*
Can I pay by credit card?	**Kan jag betala med kreditkort?** *kan yahg beh • tah • la meed kreh • deet • koart*
Can I have the receipt, please?	**Kan jag få kvittot, tack?** *kan yahg foa kvih • toht tak*
Thank you.	**Tack.** *tak*

WHERE TO EAT

Can you recommend...?	**Kan du rekommendera...?**
	kan deu reh • koh • mehn • dee • ra...
a restaurant	**en restaurang**
	ehn rehs • teu • rang
a bar	**en bar**
	ehn bahr
a cafe	**ett kafé**
	eht ka • feh
a fast-food place	**en grillbar**
	ehn grihl • bahr
a steakhouse	**ett stekhus**
	eht steek • heus
a cheap restaurant	**en billig restaurang**
	en bihl • eeg reh • stah • eu • rahng
an expensive restaurant	**en dyr restaurang**
	ehn dewr reh • stah • eu • rahng

When it comes to eating out, there are many options, ranging from fast-food stands to five-star restaurants. If you are looking for a quick bite to eat, then a **gatukök** (fast-food stand) is an easy choice. If you are looking for more traditional cuisine, this can be found at a **värdshus** (roadside restaurant), **kafé** (cafe) or **restaurang** (restaurant).

RESERVATIONS & PREFERENCES

I'd like to reserve a table…	**Jag skulle vilja boka ett bord…** *yahg <u>skuh</u> • ler <u>vihl</u> • ya <u>boh</u> • ka eht bohrd…*
for two	**för två** *furr tv**oa***
for this evening	**till ikväll** *tihl ee • <u>kvehl</u>*
for tomorrow at…	**imorgon klockan…** *ee • <u>mo</u> • ron <u>kloh</u> • kan…*
A table for two, please.	**Kan jag få ett bord för två tack.** *kan yahg f**oa** eht bohrd furr tv**oa** tak*
We have a reservation.	**Vi har bokat ett bord.** *vee hahr <u>boa</u> • kat eht bohrd*
My name is…	**Jag heter…** *yahg <u>hee</u> • tehr…*
Could we sit…?	**Får vi sitta…?** *f**oa**r vee <u>siht</u> • a…*
here/there	**här/där** *hair/dair*
outside	**ute** *<u>eu</u> • ter*
in a non-smoking area	**vid bord för icke-rökare** *veed bohrd furr <u>ee</u> • keh • <u>rur</u> • kah • rer*
by the window	**vid fönstret** *veed <u>furns</u> • treht*
in the shade	**i skuggan** *ee <u>skuh</u> • gan*
in the sun	**i solen** *ee <u>sohl</u> • ehn*
Where are the restrooms [toilets]?	**Var finns toaletten?** *vahr fihns toa • ah • <u>leh</u> • tehn*

YOU MAY HEAR...

Har ni bokat?	Do you have a
hahr nee boh • kat	reservation?
Hur många blir ni?	How many?
heur moang • a bleer nee	
Rökare eller icke-rökare?	Smoking or
rur • ka • rer ehl • ehr ee • keh • rur • ka • rer	non-smoking?
Vill ni beställa?	Are you ready
vihl nee beh • steh • la	to order?
Vad vill ni beställa?	What would
vahd vihl nee beh • steh • la	you like?
Jag kan rekommendera...	I recommend...
yahg kan reh • koh • mehn • dee • ra...	
Smaklig måltid.	Enjoy your
smahk • lihg moal • teed	meal.

HOW TO ORDER

Excuse me!	**Ursäkta!**
	eur • shehk • ta
We're ready to order.	**Vi vill gärna beställa.**
	vee vihl yair • na beh • steh • la
May I see the	**Kan jag få se vinlistan?**
	kan yahg foa see
wine list?	*veen • lihs • tan*
I'd like...	**Jag skulle vilja ha...**
	yahg skuh • ler vihl • ya hah...
a bottle of...	**en flaska...**
	ehn flahs • ka...
a glass of...	**ett glas...**
	eht glahs...

a carafe of...	**en karaff...**
	ehn kah • raf...
The menu, please.	**En meny, tack.**
	ehn meh • neu tak
Do you have...?	**Har ni...?**
	hahr nee...
a menu in English	**en meny på engelska**
	ehn meh • neu poa ehng • ehl • ska
a fixed price menu	**en meny med fast pris**
	ehn meh • neu meed fast prees
a children's menu	**en barnmeny**
	ehn bahrn • meh • neu
What do you recommend?	**Vad rekommenderar ni?**
	vahd reh • koh • mehn • dee • rar nee
What's this?	**Vad är det här?**
	vahd air dee hair
What's in it?	**Vad är det i den?**
	vahd air dee ee dehn
Is it spicy?	**Är den kryddstark?**
	air dehn kreyd • stark
I'd like...	**Jag skulle vilja ha...**
	yahg skuh • ler vihl • ya hah...
More..., please.	**Lite mer..., tack.**
	lee • teh meer...tak
With/Without...	**Med/Utan...**
	meed/eu • tan...
I can't have...	**Jag kan inte äta mat som innehåller...**
	yahg kan ihn • ter air • ta maht som ih • neh • hoal • lehr...
rare	**blodig**
	bloa • dihg
medium	**medium**
	mee • dee • uhm
well done	**genomstekt**
	ye • nom • steekt

It's to go [take away]. **Jag ska ta den med mig.**

yahg skah tah dehn meed may

For Drinks, see page 200.

YOU MAY SEE...

KUVERTAVGIFT	cover charge
FAST PRIS	fixed-price
MENY	menu
DAGENS MENY	menu of the day
DRICKS (INTE) INRÄKNAD	service (not) included
SPECIALITETER	specials

COOKING METHODS

baked	**bakad**
	bah • kad
boiled	**kokt**
	koakt
braised	**bräserad**
	braeh • seeh • rad
breaded	**panerad**
	pah • neeh • rad
creamed	**rörd**
	rurd
diced	**i bitar**
	ee bee • tar
filleted	**filead**
	fih • leeh • ad
fried	**stekt**
	steekt

grilled	**grillad**
	grihl•ad
poached	**pocherad**
	poa•sheeh•rad
roasted	**ugnstekt**
	eungn•steekt
sautéed	**stekt**
	steekt
smoked	**rökt**
	rurkt
steamed	**ångkokt**
	oang•koakt
stewed	**stuvad**
	steu•vad
stuffed	**fylld**
	fewld

DIETARY REQUIREMENTS

I am...	**Jag är...**
	yahg air...
diabetic	**diabetiker**
	dee•a•beh•tih•ker
lactose intolerant	**laktosintolerant**
	lak•toas•in•toh•leh•rant
vegetarian	**vegetarian**
	veh•geh•ta•ree•ahn
vegan	**vegan**
	veh•gahn
I'm allergic to...	**Jag är allergisk mot...**
	yahg air a•lehr•gihsk moat...
I can't eat food	**Jag kan inte äta mat som innehåller...**
that contains...	*yahg kan ihn•ter air•ta maht som ihn•neh•hoa•lehr...*

dairy	**mejeriprodukter**
	may • eh • <u>ree</u> • proh • duhk • tehr
gluten	**gluten**
	<u>glue</u> • tehn
nut	**nöt**
	n<u>ur</u>t
pork	**fläskkött**
	<u>flehsk</u> • churt
shellfish	**skaldjur**
	<u>skahl</u> • y<u>eu</u>r
spicy food	**kryddad mat**
	<u>krew</u> • dad maht
wheat	**vete**
	<u>veeh</u> • te
Is it halal/kosher?	**Är det halal/kosher?**
	air deht ha • lal/kosh • ehr
Do you have…?	**Har ni…?**
	hahr nee
skimmed milk	**lättmjölk**
	leht • myulk
whole milk	**standardmjölk**
	stahn • dardh • myulk
soya milk	**sojamjölk**
	soh • ya • myulk

DINING WITH CHILDREN

Do you have a children's menu?	**Har ni en barnmeny?**
	hahr nee ehn <u>bahrn</u> • meh • neu
Can you bring a high chair, please?	**Kan jag få en barnstol, tack?**
	kan yahg foa ehn <u>bahrn</u> • stoal tak
Where can I feed/ change the baby?	**Var kan jag mata/byta på babyn?**
	vahr kan yahg <u>mah</u> • ta/b<u>ew</u> • ta poa <u>bai</u> • been

Can you warm this?	**Kan ni värma det här?**
	kan nee <u>vair</u> • ma dee hair

For Traveling with Children, see page 134.

HOW TO COMPLAIN

How much longer will our food be?	**Hur länge till behöver vi vänta?**
	heur <u>lehng</u> • er tihl beh • <u>hur</u> • ver vee <u>vehn</u> • ta
We can't wait any longer.	**Vi kan inte vänta längre.**
	vee kan <u>ihn</u> • t'er <u>vehn</u> • ta <u>lehng</u> • rer
We're leaving.	**Vi går nu.**
	vee goar neu
That's not what I ordered.	**Det här har jag inte beställt.**
	dee hair hahr yahg <u>ihn</u> • ter beh • <u>stehlt</u>
I asked for...	**Jag beställde...**
	yahg beh • <u>stehl</u> • der...
I can't eat this.	**Jag kan inte äta det här.**
	yahg kan <u>ihn</u> • ter air • ta dee hair
This is too...	**Det här är för...**
	dee hair air furr...
cold/hot	**kallt/varmt**
	kalt/varmt
salty/spicy	**salt/kryddat**
	salt/<u>krew</u> • dat
tough/bland	**segt/smaklöst**
	sekt/<u>smahk</u> • lurst
This isn't clean/ fresh.	**Det här är inte rent/färskt.**
	dee hair air <u>ihn</u> • ter reent/fairskt

PAYING

The check [bill], please.	**Kan jag få räkningen, tack.**
	kan yahg foa <u>rairk</u> • nihng • ehn tak

We'd like to pay separately.	**Vi vill betala var för sig.**
	vee vihl beh•tah•la vahr furr say
It's all together.	**Allt tillsammans.**
	alt tihl•saa•mans
Is service included?	**Är serveringsavgiften inräknad?**
	air sehr•veeh•rihngs•afv•yihf•ten ihn•rairk•nad
What's this amount for?	**Vad står den här summan för?**
	vahd stoar dehn hair suhm•an furr
I didn't have that. I had…	**Jag åt inte det. Jag åt…**
	yahg oat ihn•ter dee yahg oat…
Can I pay by credit card?	**Kan jag betala med kreditkort?**
	kan yahg beh•tah•la meed kreh•deet•koart
Can I have an itemized bill/ a receipt?	**Kan jag få en specificerad räkning/ett kvitto?**
	kan yahg foa ehn speh•seh•fee•ee•rad rairk•nihng/eht kvih•toh
That was a very good meal.	**Det var en mycket god måltid.**
	dee vahr ehn mew•ker goad moal•teed
I've already paid.	**Jag har redan betalat.**
	yahg hahr reh•dan beh•tah•lat

MEALS & COOKING

BREAKFAST

apelsin	orange
a•pehl•seen	
bacon	bacon
bay•kohn	

bröd bread
brurd

filmjölk thick yogurt
feel • myurlk

frukostflingor (cold) cereal
fruh • kohst • flihng • or

fruktjuice fruit juice
fruhkt • yoas

grapefrukt grapefruit
grape • fruhkt

gröt (hot) cereal
grurt

havregryn oatmeal
hafv • reh • greun

honung honey
hoa • neung

kaffe... coffee...
ka • fer...

  med mjölk with milk
  meed myurlk

  med socker with sugar
  meed soh • ker

  med sötningsmedel with artificial
  meed surt • nihngs • mee • dehl sweetener

  utan koffein decaf
  eu • tan koh • feen

kallskuret cold cuts
kal • skeu • reht [charcuterie]

kokt ägg boiled egg
koakt ehg

korv sausage
kohrv

marmelad marmalade
mar • meh • lahd

mjölk	milk
myurlk	
muffin	muffin
muh • fihn	
müsli	granola [muesli]
mews • lee	
omelett	omelet
ohm • eh • leht	
ost	cheese
oast	
rostat bröd	toast
roahs • tat brurd	
småbröd	roll
smoa • brurd	
smör	butter
smur	
stekt ägg	fried egg
steekt ehg	

Frukost (breakfast) is usually served from 7:00 to 10:00 a.m. Hotels and guesthouses offer a large buffet selection of cheese, cold meat, bread, eggs, cereals and **filmjölk** (thick yogurt). **Lunch** (lunch) is served from as early as 11:00 a.m. Although many Swedes have a warm meal at lunchtime, some opt for a sandwich or a salad. This is the best time to try the **dagens rätt** (specialty of the day). **Middag** (dinner) is normally eaten early, around 6:00 or 7:00 p.m., though many restaurants continue serving until late, especially at the weekend. Many Swedes will also eat a meal later in the evening, referred to as **kvällsmål;** this evening meal usually includes sandwiches, yogurt or soup.

sylt jam
sewlt
thé tea
tee
vatten water
va • tehrn
yoghurt yogurt
yoh • geurt
ägg egg
ehg
äggröra scrambled eggs
ehg • rur • ra
äpple apple
ehp • leh

APPETIZERS

färska räkor unshelled shrimp
fair • ska räir • kohr [prawns], served
 with toast, butter
 and mayonnaise
förrätt appetizer [starter]
furr • reht
gravlax marinated salmon
grafv • lax
löjrom bleak roe, served
lurj • rohm with chopped, raw
 onions and sour
 cream and eaten on
 toast
rökt lax smoked salmon
rurkt lax
sill marinated herring
sihl

sillbricka
sihl • brih • ka
variety of
marinated herring

S.O.S. (smör, ost och sill)
*ehs oa ehs (sm**ur** oast ohk sil)*
a small plate of
marinated herring,
bread, butter and
cheese

toast skagen
toast <u>skah</u> • gehn
toast with chopped
shrimp [prawns] in
mayonnaise, topped
with bleak roe

viltpastej
<u>vihlt</u> • pa • <u>stay</u>
game pâté

SOUP

buljong
beul • <u>yong</u>
broth

fisksoppa
fihsk • <u>sop</u> • a
fish soup

grönsakssoppa
<u>grurn</u> • sahks • <u>sohp</u> • a
vegetable soup

kall soppa
kal <u>sohp</u> • a
cold soup

kycklingsoppa
<u>chewk</u> • lihng • <u>sohp</u> • a
chicken soup

kött och grönsakssoppa
<u>churt</u> • oa • <u>grurn</u> • sahk • <u>sohp</u> • a
meat and
vegetable soup

köttsoppa
<u>churt</u> • sohp • a
a hearty soup of
beef, vegetables
and dumplings

löksoppa
<u>lurk</u> • sohp • a
onion soup

nyponsoppa
<u>new</u> • pohn • sohp • a
rose-hip soup

oxsvanssoppa _oax_ • svans • _sohp_ • a	oxtail soup
potatissoppa poa • _tah_ • tihs • _sohp_ • a	potato soup
rörd soppa rurrd _sohp_ • a	cream soup
sparrissoppa _spa_ • rihs • _sohp_ • a	asparagus soup
spenatsoppa speh • _nat_ • sohp • a	a rich soup made from spinach, potatoes, milk and cream
tomatsoppa toa • _maht_ • soh • pa	tomato soup
ärtsoppa _airt_ • sohp • a	green or yellow pea soup

FISH & SEAFOOD

abborre _ah_ • bohr • er	perch
ansjovis an • _shoa_ • vees	anchovy
blåmussla _bloa_ • muhs • la	blue mussel
braxen _brak_ • sehn	sea bream
böckling _burk_ • lihng	smoked Baltic herring
fisk fihsk	fish
forell foa • _rehl_	trout
färska räkor _fairs_ • ka _rair_ • kohr	unshelled shrimp [prawns]

gravlax
grafv • lax
marinated salmon

gädda
yeh • da
sea perch

halstrad fisk
hal • strahd fihsk
grilled fish

halstrad forell med färskpotatis
hal • strad foa • rehl med fairsk • poa • tah • tihs
grilled trout with new potatoes

havsabborre
hafs • a • boh • rer
sea bass

hummer
huhm • ehr
lobster

hälleflundra
heh • leh • fleun • dra
halibut

inlagd sill
ihn • lagd sil
marinated (pickled) herring

Janssons frestelse
yahn • sons frehs • tehl • ser
casserole with potatoes and anchovies

kammussla
kam • muhs • la
scallop

kolja
kohl • ya
haddock

krabba
kra • ba
crab

kräfta
krehf • ta
crayfish

kummel
keu • mel
hake

lax
lax
salmon

löjrom *lury • rohm*	bleak roe with chopped, raw onions and sour cream; served on toast
makrill *mak • rihl*	mackerel
marulk *mahr • eulk*	monkfish
matjesill *ma • shcheh • sihl*	marinated herring
multe *muhl • ter*	mullet
mussla *muhs • la*	mussel
mört *murt*	roach (type of fish)
ostron *oas • tron*	oyster
piggvar *pihg • vahr*	turbot
rimmad lax med stuvad potatis *rihm • ahd lax meed steu • vad poa • tah • tihs*	lightly salted salmon with creamed potatoes and dill
rocka *roh • ka*	ray (type of fish)
räkor *rair • kohr*	shrimp [prawns]
röding *rur • dihng*	char
rödspätta *rurd • speh • ta*	plaice
rökt fisk *rurkt fisk*	smoked fish

rökt lax
rurkt lax
smoked salmon

rökt ål
rurkt oal
smoked eel

sardin
sar•deen
sardine

sill
sihl
herring

sillbricka
sihl•brih•ka
variety of marinated herring

sillsallad
sihl•sal•ad
beet and herring salad

sjötunga
sjur•tuhng•a
sole

skaldjur
skahl•yeur
shellfish

skaldjurssallad
skahl•yeurs•sal•ad
shellfish salad

skarpsill
skarp•sihl
herring

småsill
smoa•sihl
herring

S.O.S. (smör, ost och sill)
ehs oa ehs (smur oast ohk sihl)
small plate of marinated herring, bread, butter and cheese

stekt fisk
steekt fisk
fried fish

strömming
struhrm•ihng
sprats (small Baltic herring) filleted and sandwiched in pairs with dill and butter in the middle

strömmingsflundra
strurm • ihngs • fleun • dra

Baltic herring, filleted and sandwiched in pairs, fried, with dill and butter filling

stuvad abborre
steu • vad a • boh • rer

perch poached with onion, parsley and lemon

tonfisk
toan • fihsk

tuna

torsk
tohrshk

cod

ugnsbakad fisk
eungns • bah • kad fihsk

oven-baked fish

vitling
veet • lihng

whiting

västkustsallad
vehst • kuhst • sal • ad

west coast salad, with shrimp [prawns] and mussels

ål
oal

eel

ångkokt fisk
oang • koakt fisk

steamed fish

MEAT & POULTRY

anka
ang • ka

duck

bacon
bay • kon

bacon

biffkött
bihf • churl

beef

biffstek
bihf • steek

steak

bog
boag
shoulder (cut of meat)

broiler
broy • lehr
spring chicken

entrecote
an • treh • koat
sirloin steak

falukorv
fah • leu • kohrv
lightly spiced sausage

fasan
fa • sahn
pheasant

filé
fih • leh
filet mignon

fläsk
flehsk
pork

fläskben
flehsk • been
ham bone

fläskfilé
flehsk • fih • leh
fillet of pork

fläskkarré
flehsk • ka • reh
pork loin

fläskkorv
flehsk • kohrv
spicy, boiled pork sausage

fläsklägg
flehsk • lehg
knuckle of pork

fågel
foa • gehl
poultry

får
foar
mutton

get
yeet
kid (goat)

grillad kyckling
grihl • ahd chewk • lihng
grilled chicken

gås
goas
goose

hamburgare hamburger
ham • beur • ya • rer

hare rabbit
hah • rer

hjort deer
yohrt

isterband sausage of pork,
ihs • tehr • band barley and beef

kalkon turkey
kal • koan

kallskuret cold cuts
kal • skeu • reht [charcuterie]

kalops beef stew
ka • lohps

kalvkött veal
kalv • churt

kalvsylta cold veal in jelly
kalv • sewl • ta

karré tenderloin
ka • reh

kokt skinka boiled ham
koakt shihng • ka

korv sausage
kohrv

kotlett cutlet
koht • lehtt

kyckling chicken
chewk • lihng

kycklingbröst chicken breast
chewk • lihng • brurst

kycklinglever chicken liver
chewk • lihng • lee • vehr

kåldomar med gräddsås och lingon chopped [minced]
koal • dohl • mar meed grehd • soas ohk meat and rice

lihng • ohn — stuffed in cabbage leaves

kött
churt — meat

köttbulle
churt • buh • ler — meatball

köttfärs
churt • fairs — chopped [minced] beef

lamm
lamm — lamb

lammgryta
lamm • grew • ta — lamb stew

lever
lee • vehr — liver

leverpastej
lee • vehr pa • stay — liver pâté

lägg
lehg — shank (top of leg)

lövbiff
lurv • bihf — fried, thinly sliced beef, with onions

medaljong
meh • dal • yong — small fillet of cut meat

njure
nyeu • rer — kidney

nötkött
nurt • churt — red meat

oxkött
oax • churt — ox

oxrullad
oax • reu • lahd — braised roll of beef

oxsvans
oax • svans — oxtail

pannbiff
pan • bihf — beef patty

prinskorv _prihns_ • _kohrv_	small pork sausage
pärlhöns _pairl_ • _hurns_	guinea fowl
ragu _ra_ • _guh_	beef stew
rapphöna _rap_ • _hurna_	partridge
ren _reen_	reindeer
renstek med svampsås _reen_ • _steek meed svamp_ • _soas_	roast reindeer with mushroom sauce
revbensspjäll _reev_ • _beens_ • _spehl_	spareribs
rostbiff _rohst_ • _bihf_	roast beef
rumpstek _ruhmp_ • _steek_	rump steak
rådjur _roa_ • _yeur_	venison
rådjursstek _roa_ • _yeur_ • _steek_	roast of venison
rökt renstek _rurkt reen_ • _steek_	smoked reindeer
rökt skinka _rurkt shihng_ • _ka_	smoked ham
sadel _sah_ • _dehl_	saddle (cut of meat)
salamikorv _sa_ • _lah_ • _mee_ • _kohrv_	salami
schnitzel _shniht_ • _sehl_	escallope
sillsallad _sihl_ • _sal_ • _ad_	beet and herring salad

sjömansbiff
shur•mans•bihf

casserole of fried beef, onions and potatoes, braised in beer

skinka
shihng•ka

ham

spädgris
spaird•grees

an unweaned piglet

stekt kyckling
steekt chewk•lihng

fried chicken (not breaded)

T-benstek
tee•been•steek

T-bone steak

tunga
tuhng•a

tongue (cow)

ⓘ

If you've never heard of typical Swedish food, you may at least be familiar with the famous **smörgåsbord** — it is a buffet meal on a grand scale, presented on a large, beautifully decorated table. You start at one end of the table, usually the one with the cold seafood dishes, marinated herring, **Janssons frestelse** (literally, Jansson's temptation, a potato and anchovies casserole) and salad. Then you work your way through the cold meat, meatballs, sausage, omelets and vegetables. Finally, you end at the cheeseboard and desserts. You're welcome to start all over again; the price is set, and you can eat as much as you like. You will find that the Swedes tend to drink **akvavit** (aquavit) or beer with the feast, although an accompanying glass of wine is becoming more common for those who find **akvavit** too strong.

At Christmas time, the **smörgåsbord** becomes a **julbord** (Christmas buffet), popular in homes and restaurants alike.

ugnsstekt kyckling	roast chicken
eungn • steekt _chewk_ • lihng	
vaktel	quail
vak • tehl	
varmkorv	hot dog
varm • kohrv	
wienerschnitzel	breaded veal cutlet
vee • nehr • shniht • sehl	
vildand	wild duck
vihld • and	
vilt	game
vihlt	
älg	moose
ehly	
älgfilé	fillet of moose
ehly • fih • _leh_	
älgstek	moose roast
ehly • steek	
älgstek med svampsås	roast moose with
ehly • steek meed _svamp_ • soas	mushroom sauce

VEGETABLES & STAPLES

avokado	avocado
a • voh • _kah_ • doa	
basilika	basil
ba • sih • _lee_ • ka	
blandsallad	mixed salad
bland • sal • ad	
blomkål	cauliflower
bloam • koal	
bouquet garni	mixed herbs
boh • _keh_ gar • _nee_	
böna...	...bean
bur • na...	

bond	broad
boand	
bryt	kidney
br<u>ew</u>t	
grön	green
gr<u>urn</u>	
vax	butter
<u>*vax*</u>	
broccoli	broccoli
<u>*broh*</u> • *koh* • *lee*	
brysselkål	Brussel sprout
<u>*brew*</u> • *sehl* • *koal*	
bröd	bread
br<u>urd</u>	
bönskott	bean sprout
<u>*burn*</u> • *skoht*	
champinjon	mushroom
sham • *pihn* • <u>*yoan*</u>	
chilipeppar	chili pepper
<u>*shee*</u> • *lih* • <u>*peh*</u> • *par*	
dragon	tarragon
dra • <u>*goan*</u>	
endiv	endive
an • <u>*deev*</u>	
fullkornsmjöl	whole wheat flour
<u>*fuhl*</u> • *kohrns* • *my<u>url</u>*	
fänkål	fennel
<u>*fehn*</u> • *koal*	
färskpotatis	new potato
<u>*fairsk*</u> • *poa* • <u>*tah*</u> • *this*	
gräslök	chive
<u>*grairs*</u> • *l<u>ur</u>k*	
grön paprika	green pepper
gr<u>urn</u> <u>*pah*</u> • *pree* • *ka*	

grönsak
grurn • sahk

vegetable

grönsallad
grurn • sal • ad

lettuce

gurka
geur • ka

cucumber

haricots verts
ar • ee • koh • vair

green bean

honung
hoa • neung

honey

ingefära
ih • ng • eh • fai • ra

ginger

kanel
ka • neel

cinnamon

kantarell
kan • ta • rehl

chanterelle
mushroom

kapris
ka • prees

caper

kikärta
cheek • air • ta

chickpea

kokt potatis
koakt poa • tah • tihs

boiled potato

kronärtskocka
kroan • airts • koh • ka

artichoke

kryddpeppar
krewd • peh • par

allspice

kummin
keu • meen

caraway

kål
koal

cabbage

kålrot
koal • roht

turnip

källkrasse
chehl • kra • ser

watercress

körvel _chur • vehl_	chervil
lagerblad _lah • gehr • blahd_	bay leaf
lins _lihns_	lentil
lök _lurk_	onion
majs _mays_	sweet corn
mjöl _myurl_	flour
morot _moa • roht_	carrot
muskot _muhs • koht_	nutmeg
mynta _mewn • ta_	mint (herb)
nejlika _nay • lih • ka_	clove
nudel _neu • dehl_	noodle
olja och vinäger _oal • ya ohk vee • nai • gehr_	oil and vinegar
palsternacka _pal • stehr • na • ka_	parsnip
paprika _pah • prih • ka_	pepper (fresh)
pasta _pas • ta_	pasta
persilja _pair • shihl • ya_	parsley
potatis _poa • tah • tihs_	potato

potatissallad	potato salad
poa • _tah_ • tihs • _sal_ • ad	
pumpa	pumpkin
puhm • pa	
purjolök	leek
peur • yoh • l**ur**k	
ris	rice
rees	
rosmarin	rosemary
roas • ma • _reen_	
rova	turnip
roa • va	
rädisa	radish
raid • dih • sa	
röd paprika	sweet red pepper
r**ur**d _pah_ • pree • ka	
rödbeta	beet
_r**ur**d_ • bee • ta	
rödkål	red cabbage
_r**ur**d_ • k**oa**l	
salladshuvud	head of lettuce
sal • ads • heu • vuhd	
saltgurka	salted, pickled
salt • geur • ka	gherkin
salvia	sage
sal • _vee_ • a	
schalottenlök	shallot [spring
sha • _loh_ • tehn • l**ur**k	onion]
selleri	celery
seh • leh • _ree_	
sirap	syrup
seh • rap	
skogssvamp	field mushroom
skoags • svamp	

smör
smurr
butter

sockerärta
soh • kehr • air • ta
sugar snap pea [mangetout]

sparris
spar • ihs
asparagus

spenat
speh • naht
spinach

squash
skoawsh
squash (vegetable)

svamp
svamp
mushroom

sötpotatis
surt • poa • tah • tihs
sweet potato

timjan
tihm • yan
thyme

tomat
toa • maht
tomato

tomater och lök
toa • mah • ter ohk lurk
tomato and onion salad

vanilj
va • nihly
vanilla

vattenkrasse
kra • ser
watercress

vetemjöl
vee • teh • mjurl
wheat flour (regular)

vild champinjon
vihl • da sham • pihn • yoan
wild mushroom

vitkål
veet • koal
white cabbage

vitlök
veet • lurk
garlic

vårlök
voar • lurk
shallot [spring onion]

zucchini
seu • kee • nee

zucchini [courgette]

äggplanta
ehg • plan • ta

eggplant
[aubergine]

ärta
air • ta

peas

ättiksgurka
eh • tiks • geur • kah

pickled gherkin

FRUIT

ananas
an • a • nas

pineapple

apelsin
a • pehl • seen

orange

aprikos
a • prih • koas

apricot

banan
ba • nahn

banana

bigarrå
bih • ga • roa

sweet morello
cherry

björnbär
byurn • bair

blackberry

blå vindruva
bloa veen • dreu • va

black grape

blåbär
bloa • bair

blueberry

citron
see • troan

lemon

dadel
dahd • ehl

date

enbär
een • bair

juniper berry

fikon
fee • kohn

fig

frukt	fruit
fruhkt	
grapefrukt	grapefruit
grape • fruhkt	
grön vindruva	green grape
grurn veen • dreu • va	
hallon	raspberry
hal • ohn	
hasselnöt	hazelnut
ha • sehl • nurt	
hjortron	cloudberry
yoahr • tron	
jordgubbe	strawberry
yoard • guh • ber	
jordnöt	peanut
yoard • nurt	
katrinplommon	prune
ka • treen • ploa • mohn	
kiwifrukt	kiwi
kee • vee • fruhkt	
kokosnöt	coconut
koa • kos • nurt	
krusbär	gooseberry
kreus • bair	
körsbär	cherry
churs • bair	
lingon	lingonberry
lihng • ohn	
mandarin	tangerine/
man • da reen	mandarin orange
mandel	almond
man • dehl	
(vatten)melon	(water)melon
(va • tehrn)meh • loan	

mullbär — mulberry
muhl • bair

nektarin — nectarine
nehk • ta • reen

oliv — olive
o • leev

persika — peach
pairsh • ih • ka

plommon — plum
plohm • on

pomegranat äpple — pomegranate
pom • eh • gra • naht • ehp • leh

päron — pear
pai • rohn

rabarber — rhubarb
rah • bar • behr

russin — raisin
ruh • sihn

röd vinbär — red currant
rurd veen • bair

smultron — wild strawberry
smeul • trohn

sultana — sultana raisin
suhl • tahn • a

svart vinbär — black currant
svart veen • bair

valnöt — walnut
vahl • nurt

vinbär — currant
veen • bair

vindruva — grape
veen • dreu • va

äpple — apple
ehp • leh

CHEESE

fårost
foar • oast
ewe's milk cheese

getost
yeet • oast
goat cheese

grevé
greh • vee
a semi-hard cheese similar to gouda and emmentaler

herrgårdsost
hehr • goards • oast
a semi-hard cheese with large holes and a nutty flavor

kryddost
krewd • oast
a sharp, strong cheese with caraway seeds

mesost
mees • oast
a soft, sweet, yellowish whey cheese

mjukost
myeuk • oast
soft cheese

ost
oast
cheese

ostbricka
oast • brih • ka
cheese plate

prästost
prehst • oast
hard cheese with a strong, rich flavor

svecia
sveh • see • a
semi-hard cheeses

västerbotten
vehs • tehr • boh • tehrn
a sharp, tangy, hard and very strong cheese from the north of Sweden

ädelost
air • dehl • oast

a blue cheese with a sharp taste, similar to Roquefort

DESSERT

efterrätt
ehf • tehr • reht

dessert

friterad camembert med hjortronsylt
free • _tee_ • rad cam • ehm • _behrt_ meed _yoh_ • tron • sewlt

deep-fried camembert with cloudberry jam

fruktsallad
fruhkt • sal • ad

fruit salad

glass
glas

ice cream

jordgubbar med grädde
yoard • guhb • ar meed _greh_ • deh

strawberries and cream

kaka
kah • ka

cake

mandeltårta
man • dehl • _toar_ • ta

almond tart

marängsviss
mah • _rehng_ • svis

meringue with whipped cream and chocolate sauce

mjuk pepparkaka
myeuk peh • par • kah • ka

soft ginger cake

ostkaka
oast • _kah_ • ka

traditional southern Sweden curd cake

tårta
toarta

sponge-based fruit or cream cake

våffla (med sylt och grädde)
vohf • la meed sewlt ohk _greh_ • der

waffle (with jam and whipped cream)

äppelpaj
_eh_ • pehl • _pay_

apple tart

äppelkaka	apple cake
eh • pehl • kah • ka	
äppelring	apple fritter
ehp • ehl • rihng	

SAUCES & CONDIMENTS

peppar	pepper
peh • par	
salt	salt
salt	
senap	mustard
see • nap	
socker	sugar
soh • kehr	
sötningsmedel	artificial sweetener
surt • nihngs • mee • dehl	
ketchup	ketchup
keht • shuhp	

AT THE MARKET

Where are the carts [trolleys]/baskets?	**Var finns shoppingvagnarna/ shoppingkorgarna?**
	vahr fihns shoh • pihng • vagn • nar • na/ shoh • pihng • kohr • yar • na
Where is/are...?	**Var finns...?** *vahr fihns...*
I'd like some of this/that.	**Jag skulle vilja ha lite av det här/ det där.**
	yahg skuh • ler vihl • ya hah lee • teh afv dee hair/dee dair
Can I taste it?	**Får jag smaka?**
	foar yahg smah • ka
I'd like...	**Jag skulle vilja ha...**
	yahg skuh • ler vihl • ya hah...

a kilo/half-kilo of...	**ett kilo/halvt kilo...**
	eht chee • loh/halft chee • loh...
a liter/half-liter of...	**en liter/halv liter...**
	ehn lee • ter/halv lee • ter...
a piece of...	**en bit av...**
	ehn beet afv...
a slice of...	**en skiva av...**
	ehn shee • va afv...
More/Less than that.	**Mer/Mindre än det där.**
	meer/mihn • dreh ehn dee dair
How much does it cost?	**Hur mycket kostar det?**
	heur mew • ker kos • tar dee
Where do I pay?	**Var kan jag betala?**
	vahr kan yahg beh • tah • la
Can I have a bag?	**Kan jag få en påse?**
	kan yahg foa ehn poa • seh
I'm being helped.	**Tack, jag har fått hjälp.**
	tak yahg hahr foat yehlp

YOU MAY HEAR...

Kan jag hjälpa er? — Can I help you?
kan yahg yehl • pa eer

Vad vill ni beställa? — What would you like?
vahd vihl nee beh • steh • la

Något annat? — Anything else?
noa • goht an • nat

Det kostar...kronor. — That's...kronor.
dee kos • tar...kroa • nohr

Measurements in Europe are metric — and that applies to the weight of food too. If you tend to think in pounds and ounces, it's worth brushing up on what the equivalent is before you go shopping for fruit and veg in markets and supermarkets. Five hundred grams, or half a kilo, is a common quantity to order, and that converts to just over a pound (17.65 ounces, to be precise).

Although Sweden still has many small, specialty shops, they are slowly giving way to **köpcentrum** (shopping centers), especially in larger towns. You can still find markets that sell fresh fruit and vegetables as well as flowers and some handicrafts. **Julmarknaden** (the traditional Christmas market) in Stockholm is reminiscent of times gone by. Supermarkets can be found in most large towns, cities and suburbs. **Närbutiker** (corner shops), as well as **Pressbyrån** (newsstand chain) sell a good range of food. In Stockholm, **Östermalmshallen** and **Hötorgshallen** (market halls) sell fresh meat — including reindeer and moose — fish and poultry. Swedes enjoy a variety of fish and seafood, and one will find a good selection in most restaurants and supermarkets. If you visit Sweden in August, you will no doubt enjoy a **kräftkalas** (crayfish party). There is not much meat on a crayfish, but when helped down with a few glasses of **akvavit** (aquavit) and some salad and cheese, it makes for an unforgettable evening.

IN THE KITCHEN

bottle opener	**flasköppnare**	_flask_ • eup • na • rehr
bowl	**djup tallrik**	y_eu_p _tal_ • rihk
can opener	**konservöppnare**	kohn • _sehrv_ • urp • nah • rer
corkscrew	**korkskruv**	_kohrk_ • skr_eu_v
cup	**kopp**	kohp
fork	**gaffel**	_gahf_ • ehl
frying pan	**stekpanna**	_steek_ • pan • na
glass	**glas**	glahs
knife	**kniv**	kneev
measuring cup/ spoon	**mått/måttsked**	moat/_moat_ • sheed
napkin	**servett**	sehr • _vehtt_
plate	**tallrik**	_tal_ • rihk
pot	**gryta**	_grew_ • ta
saucepan	**kastrull**	kas • _truhl_
spatula	**steekspade**	_steek_ • spah • der
spoon	**sked**	sheed

DRINKS

NEED TO KNOW

May I see the wine list/drink menu?	**Kan jag få se vinlistan/ drinklistan?**
	kan yahg foa see veen • lihs • tan/ drihnk • lihs • tan
What do you recommend?	**Vad rekommenderar ni?**
	vahd reh • koh • mehn • dee • rar nee
I'd like a bottle/glass of red/white wine.	**Jag skulle vilja ha en flaska/ett glas rött/ vitt vin.**
	yahg skuh • ler vihl • ya hah ehn flas • ka/ eht glahs ruhrt/viht veen
The house wine, please.	**Husets vin, tack.**
	heu • sehts veen tak
Another bottle/glass, please.	**En flaska/Ett glas till, tack.**
	ehn flas • ka/eht glahs tihl tak
I'd like a local beer.	**Jag skulle vilja ha en öl från trakten.**
	yahg skuh • ler vihl • ya hah ehn url fron trak • tehn
Let me buy you a drink.	**Får jag bjuda på en drink.**
	foar yahg byeu • da poa ehn drihnk
Cheers!	**Skål!** *skoal*
A coffee/tea, please.	**En kopp kaffe/te, tack.**
	ehn kohp ka • fer/tee tak
Black.	**Svart.**
	Svart
With...	**Med...**
	meed...

milk	**mjölk**
	myuhlk
sugar	**socker**
	soh • kehr
artificial	**sötningsmedel**
sweetener	*surt • nihngs • mee • dehl*
decaf	**utan koffein** *eu • tan koh • feen*
…, please.	**…, tack.**
	…tak
Juice	**Juice**
	yoas
Soda	**sodavatten**
	soa • da • va • tehrn
Sparkling water	**Vatten med kolsyra**
	va • tehrn meed koal • sew • ra
Still water	**Vatten utan kolsyra**
	va • tehrn eu • tan koal • sew • ra
Is the tap water safe to drink?	**Kan man dricka kranvattnet?**
	kan man drih • ka krahn • vat • neht

NON-ALCOHOLIC DRINKS

alkoholfri dryck	non-alcoholic drink
al • ko • hoal • free drewk	
ananasjuice	pineapple juice
an • a • nas • yoas	
apelsinjuice	orange juice
a • pehl • seen • yoas	
cola	cola
koa • la	
fruktjuice	fruit juice
fruhkt • yoas	

juice	juice
yoas	
kaffe	coffee
ka•fer	
läsk	soft drink
lehsk	
milkshake	milk shake
milk•shake	
mineralvatten	mineral water
mihn•eh•rahl•va•tehrn	
mjölk	milk
myurlk	
saft	squash (fruit
saft	cordial)
sockerdricka	lemonade
soh•kehr•drih•ka	
sodavatten	soda water
soa•da•va•tehrn	

For afternoon tea (usually enjoyed with lemon) or coffee you can do no better than the typical Swedish **konditori** (patisserie or coffee shop). Help yourself to as many cups as you like while indulging in a slice of **prinsesstårta** (sponge cake with cream and custard, covered with green marzipan), **mazarin** (almond tart, topped with icing) or a **wienerbröd** (Danish pastry). Try **saffransbullar** (saffron buns) and **pepparkakor** (ginger cookies) at Christmas. Most **konditori** are self-service, but some of the more elegant ones and those in hotels provide full service. Coffee is definitely the national drink, and it is always freshly brewed. It is commonly drunk black, but ask for **mjölk** (milk) or **grädde** (cream) if you like it that way.

thé med mjölk/citron
tee meed myurlk/
see • troan

tea with milk/lemon

tomatjuice
toa • maht • yoas

tomato juice

tonic
toh • nihk

tonic water

varmchoklad
varm shoa • klahd

hot chocolate

vatten med/utan kolsyra
va • tehrn meed/ eu • tan koal • sew • ra

sparkling/still water

YOU MAY HEAR...

Får jag bjuda på en drink?
foar yahg
bjeu • da pao ehn drink

Can I buy you a drink?

Med mjölk/socker?
meed myurlk/soh • ker

With milk/sugar?

Vatten med/utan kolsyra?
va • tehrn meed/ eu • tan koal • sew • ra

Sparkling/Still water?

APERITIFS, COCKTAILS & LIQUEURS

akvavit
a • kva • veet

aquavit, the famous Swedish grain- or potato-based spirit

cognac
kohn • yak

brandy

gin
jihn

gin

glögg
glurg

mulled wine with port and spices, served hot

herrgårdsakvavit
hair • goards • a • kva • veet

aquavit, flavored with caraway seeds and whisky

likör
lih • kurr

liqueur

portvin
port • veen

port

punsch
peunsh

sweet liqueur

rom
rohm

rum

sherry
sheh • ree

sherry

skåne
skoa • ner

aquavit, flavored with aniseed and caraway seeds

sprit
spreet

spirits

vermouth
vehr • meutt

vermouth

vodka...
vod • ka...

vodka...

med is
meed ees

on the rocks [with ice]

med tonic
meed toh • nihk

with tonic water

med vatten
meed va • tehrn

with water

whisky
vihs • kee

whisky

BEER

burköl *buhrk • url*	canned beer
fatöl *faht • url*	draft [draught]
lättöl *leht • url*	light beer
öl på flaska *url poa fla • ska*	bottled beer local/ imported
utan alkohol *uh • tan al • koh • hohl*	non-alcoholic

Beer is probably the most popular alcoholic drink in Sweden, and there are many good Swedish breweries. Beer with an alcohol content above 3%, called **starköl**, can only be bought in **Systembolaget** (state liquor store); **lättöl** and **folköl**, which are below 3% alcohol content, can be bought in grocery stores and supermarkets. You will find many well known international beers, but the most common are Carlsberg, Heineken and Swedish brews such as Pripps and Falcon.

WINE

dessertvin *deh • sair • veen*	dessert wine
husets vin *heu • sehts veen*	house wine
mousserande *moa • see • ran • der*	sparkling

rosé
roh • seh
blush [rosé]

rött
ruhrt
red

sött
suhrt
sweet

torrt
tohrt
dry

vitt
viht
white

champagne
shahm • pany
champagne

ON THE MENU

abborre
ah • bohr • er
perch

akvavit
a • kva • veet
aquavit, the famous Swedish grain- or potato-based spirit

alkoholfri dryck
al • ko • hoal • free drewk
non-alcoholic drink

ananas
an • a • nas
pineapple

ananasjuice
an • a • nas • yoas
pineapple juice

anka
ang • ka
duck

ansjovis
an • shoa • vees
anchovy

apelsin
a • pehl • seen
orange

apelsinjuice
a • pehl • seen • yoas

orange juice

aprikos
a • prih • koas

apricot

avokado
a • voh • kah • doa

avocado

bacon
bay • kon

bacon

bakelse
bah • kehl • sehr

piece of cake

bakverk
bahk • verk

pastry

banan
ba • nahn

banana

basilika
ba • sih • lee • ka

basil

biffkött
bihf • churt

beef

biffstek
bif • steek

steak

bigarrå
bih • ga • roa

sweet morello
cherry

bit
beet

slice

björnbär
byurn • bair
blackberry

blandade
blan • da • der
assorted

blandade grönsaker
blan • da • der
grurn • sah • kehr
mixed vegetables

blandade kryddor
blan • da • der krew • dohr
mixed herbs

blandade nötter
blan • da • der nur • tehr
assorted nuts

blandsallad
bland • sal • ad
mixed salad

blodig
bloa • dihg
rare

blomkål
bloam • koal
cauliflower

blå vindruva
bloa veen • dreu • va
black grape

blåbär
bloa • bair
blueberry

blåbärssylt
bloa • bairs • sewlt
blueberry jam

blåmussla
bloa • muhs • la
blue mussel

bog
boag
shoulder (cut of meat)

bondböna
boand • bur • nohr
broad bean

bordsvin
boards • veen
table wine

bouquet garni
boh • keh gar • nee
mixed herbs

braxen
brak • sehn
sea bream

broccoli
broh • loh • lee
broccoli

broiler
broy • lehr
spring chicken

brylépudding
brew • lee • peu • dihng
crème brulee

brysselkål
brew • sehl • koal
brussel sprout

brytböna
brewt • bur • na
kidney bean

brännvin
brehn • veen
aquavit, grain or potato based spirit

bröd
brurd
bread

brödsmulor
brurd • smeu • lohr
bread crumbs

bröst
brurst
breast

buljong
buhl • yong
broth

bulle
buh • ler
bun

burköl
buhrk • url
canned beer

bål
boal
punch

böckling
burk • lihng
smoked herring

böna
bur • na
bean [pulses]

bönskott
burn • skoht
bean sprout

champinjon
sham • pihn • yoan
mushroom

chilipeppar
shee • lih • peh • par

chili pepper

chips
shihps

potato chips
[crisps]

choklad
shoa • klahd

chocolate

citron
see • troan

lemon

citronjuice
see • troan • yoas

lemon juice

cognac
kohn • yak

brandy

cola
koa • la

cola

dadel
dahd • ehl

date

dagens meny
dah • gehns meh • neu

menu of the day

dagens rätt
dah • gehns rairtt

speciality of the
day

dessertvin
deh • sair • veen

dessert wine

dillsås
dihl • soas

dill sauce

dragon
dra • goan

tarragon

dryck med alkohol
drewk meed al • ko • hoal

alcoholic drink

efterrätt
ehf • tehr • rairt

dessert

en halv flaska
ehn halv fla • ska

half bottle

enbär
een • bair

juniper berry

endiv
an • deev

endive

entrecote
an • treh • koa

sirloin steak

falukorv
fah • leu • kohrv

lightly spiced
sausage

fasan
fa • sahn

pheasant

fatöl
faht • url

draft [draught] beer

fikon
fee • kohn

fig

filé
fih • leh

filet mignon

filmjölk
feel • mjurlk

thick yogurt

fisk
fihsk

fish

fisk och skaldjur
fihsk • ohk • skahl • yeur

fish and seafood

fisksoppa
fihsk • sop • a

fish soup

fläsk
flehsk

pork

fläskben
flehsk • been

ham bone

fläskfilé
flehsk • fih • leh

fillet of pork

fläskkarré
flehsk • ka • reh

pork loin

fläskkorv
flehsk • kohrv

spicy, boiled pork
sausage

fläsklägg
flehsk • lehg

knuckle of pork

fläskpannkaka _flehsk • pan • kah • ka_	thick pancake filled with bacon
forell _foa • rehl_	trout
franskbröd _fransk • brurd_	French bread
friterad camembert med hjortronsylt _free • tee • rad cam • ehm • behrt meed_ _yoh • tron • sewlt_	deep-fried Camembert with cloudberry jam
frukost _fruh • kohst_	breakfast
frukostflingor _fruhkost • flihng • ohr_	(cold) cereal
frukt _fruhkt_	fruit
fruktjuice _fruhkt • yoas_	fruit juice
fruktsallad _fruhkt • sal • ad_	fruit salad
fullkornsmjöl _fuhl • kohrns • myurl_	whole wheat flour
fylld (med) _fewld (meed)_	stuffed (with)
fylld oliv _fewld o • leev_	stuffed olive
fylligt _few • liht_	full-bodied (wine)
fågel _foa • gehl_	poultry
får _foar_	mutton
fårost _foar • oast_	ewe's milk cheese
fänkål _fehn • koal_	fennel

färsk (frukt)
fehrsk (fruhkt)
fresh (fruit)

färsk fikon
fairsk fee•kohn
fresh fig

färska räkor
fairs•ka rair•kohr
unshelled shrimp [prawns]

färskpotatis
fairsk•poa•tah•tihs
new potato

förlorat ägg
furr•loa•rat ehg
poached egg

förrätt
furr•rairt
appetizer [starter]

garnering
gar•nee•rihng
garnish

gelé
sheh•leh
jelly

get
yeet
kid (goat)

getost
yeet•oast
goat cheese

gin
jihn
gin

glass
glas
ice cream

glutenfritt
glue•tehn•friht
gluten free

glögg
glurg
mulled wine with port and spices, served hot

grapefrukt
grahp•fruhkt
grapefruit

gratinerad
gra•tih•nee•rad
au gratin

gratäng
gra•tehng
casserole

gravlax
grafv • lax
marinated salmon

grevé
greh • veh
semi-hard cheese

grillad kyckling
grihl • ahd chewk • lihng
grilled chicken

grillspett
grihl • speht
skewer

gryta
grew • ta
pot roast, stew or casserole

grädde
greh • der
cream

gräddfil
grehd • feel
sour cream

gräslök
grairs • lurk
chive

grön böna
grur • na bur • na
green bean

grön paprika
grurn pah • pree • ka
green pepper

grön vindruva
grurn veen • dreu • va
green grape

grönsak
grurn • sahk
vegetable

grönsakssoppa
grurn • sahks • sohp • a
vegetable soup

grönsallad
grurn • sal • ad
green salad

gröt
grurt
(hot) cereal

gurka
geur • ka
cucumber

gås
goas
goose

gädda _yeh_ • da	sea perch
hallon _hal_ • ohn	raspberry
halstrad fisk _hal_ • strahd fihsk	grilled fish
halstrad forell med färskpotatis _hal_ • strad foa • _rehl_ med _fairsk_ • poa • _tah_ • this	grilled trout with new potatoes
hamburgare _ham_ • beur • ya • rer	hamburger
hare _hah_ • rer	rabbit
haricots verts ar • ee • koh • _vair_	string beans
hasselbackspotatis _ha_ • sehl • baks • poa • _tah_ • tihs	oven-baked potato, coated in bread crumbs
hasselnöt _ha_ • sehl • nurt	hazelnut
havre _hafv_ • rer	oats
havregryn _hafv_ • reh • greun	oatmeal
havsabborre _hafs_ • a • boh • rer	sea bass
hemlagad _hehm_ • lah • gad	homemade
herrgårdsakvavit _hair_ • goards • a • kva • _veet_	aquavit flavored with caraway seeds and whisky
herrgårdsost _hehr_ • goards • oast	semi-hard cheese with a nutty flavor
hett _heht_	hot (temperature)

hjort
yohrt
deer

hjortron
yoahr • tron
cloudberry

hjortron sylt
yoar • trohn • sewlt
cloudberry jam

honung
hoa • neung
honey

hovmästarsås
hoav • mehs • tar • soas
dill sauce

hummer
huhm • ehr
lobster

husets specialitet
heu • sehts speh • sih • al • ee • teet
specialty of the house

husets vin
heu • sehts veen
house wine

huvudrätt
heu • vuhd • rait
main course

hårdkokt ägg
hoard • kohkt ehg
hard-boiled egg

hårt bröd
hoart brurd
crispbread

hälleflundra
heh • leh • fleun • dra
halibut

ingefära
ih • ng • eh • fai • ra
ginger

inlagd i ättika (vinäger)
ihn • lahgd ee eh • tih • ka
marinated in vinegar

inlagd sill
ihn • lahgd sil
marinated (pickled) herring

is
ees
ice

isterband
ihs • tehr • band
sausage of pork, barley and beef

Janssons frestelse
yahn • sons _frehs_ • tehl • ser
casserole with potatoes and anchovies

jordgubbar med grädde
yoard • guhb • ar meed _greh_ • deh
strawberries and cream

jordgubbe
yoard • guh • ber
strawberry

jordnöt
yoard • nurt
peanut

juice
yoas
juice

julbord
yeul • board
buffet of hot and cold Swedish specialties served at Christmas time

kaffe
_ka_ • fer
coffee

kaka
kah • ka
cake

kalkon
kal • _koan_
turkey

kall soppa
kal _sohp_ • a
cold soup

kallskuret
kal • sk_eu_ • reht
cold cuts

kalops
ka • _lohps_
beef stew

kalvbräss
kalv • brehs
sweetbread

kalvkött
kalv • churt
veal

kalvsylta
kalv • s_ew_l • ta
cold veal in jelly

kammussla
kam • muhs • la
scallop

kanderad frukt candied fruit
kan • deeh • rahd fruhkt

kanel cinnamon
ka • neel

kantarell chanterelle
kan • ta • rehl mushroom

kapris caper
ka • prees

karaff carafe
ka • raff

karameller candy [sweets]
ka • ra • mehl • ehr

karré tenderloin
ka • reh

katrinplommon prune
ka • treen • ploa • mohn

kex cookie [biscuit]
kehx

kikärta chickpea
cheek • air • ta

kiwifrukt kiwi
kee • vee • fruhkt

klimp dumpling
klihmp

kokosnöt coconut
koa • kos • nurt

kokt katrinplommon stewed prune
koakt ka • treen • ploa • mohn

kokt potatis boiled potato
koakt poa • tah • tihs

kokt skinka boiled ham
koakt shihng • ka

kokt ägg boiled egg
koakt ehg

kolja _kohl_ • ya	haddock
kolsyrad _koal_ • sew • rad	carbonated
kompott kom • _poht_	stewed fruit
konserverad frukt kon • ser • _vee_ • rad fruhkt	canned fruit
korv kohrv	sausage
kotlett koht • _lehtt_	cutlet
krabba _kra_ • ba	crab
kronärtskocka _kroan_ • airts • koh • ka	artichoke
kroppkaka _kropp_ • kah • ka	potato dumpling, filled with bacon and onions
krusbär _kreus_ • bair	gooseberry
krydda _krew_ • da	spice
kryddad _krew_ • dad	spicy
kryddad pepparsås _krew_ • dahd _peh_ • par • _soas_	hot pepper sauce
kryddost _krewd_ • oast	sharp, strong cheese with caraway seeds
kryddpeppar _krewd_ • peh • par	allspice
kryddstarkt _krewd_ • starkt	spicy

kräfta
krehf•ta
crayfish

kummel
keu•mel
hake

kummin
keu•meen
caraway

kvark
kvark
fresh curd cheese

kyckling
chewk•lihng
chicken

kycklingbröst
chewk•lihng•brurst
chicken breast

kycklinglever
chewk•lihng•lee•vehr
chicken liver

kycklingsoppa
chewk•lihng•sohp•a
chicken soup

kyld dryck
chewl drewk
cold drink

kylt
chewlt
chilled (wine, etc.)

kål
koal
cabbage

kåldolmar
koal•dohl•mar
cabbage leaves stuffed with chopped [minced] meat and rice

kålrot
koal•roht
turnip

källkrasse
chehl•kra•se
watercress

körsbär
churs•bair
cherry

körvel
chur•vehl
chervil

kött
churt
meat

kött och grönsakssoppa
churt • oa • grurn • sahk • sohp • a
meat and vegetable soup soup

köttbulle
churt • buh • ler
meatball

köttfärs
churt • fairs
chopped [minced] beef

köttsoppa
churt • sohp • a
beef and vegetable soup with dumplings

köttsås
churt • soas
meat sauce

lagerblad
lah • gehr • blahd
bay leaf

lageröl
lah • ger • url
lager

lamm
lamm
lamb

lammgryta
lamm • grew • ta
lamb stew

landgång
land • goang
long open-faced sandwich

lax
lax
salmon

lever
lee • vehr
liver

leverpastej
lee • vehr pa • stay
liver pâté

lingon
lihng • ohn
lingonberry

lingonsylt
lihng • ohn • sewlt
lingonberry jam

lins
lihns
lentil

likör
lih • kurr
liqueur

lägg
lehg
shank (top of leg)

läsk
lehsk
soft drink

lättöl
leht • ur
light beer

löjrom
lury • rohm
bleak roe with chopped, raw onions and sour cream; served on toast

lök
lurk
onion

löksoppa
lurk • sohp • a
onion soup

lövbiff
lurv • bihf
fried, thinly sliced beef, with onions

majonnäs
may • oha • nairs
mayonnaise

majs
mays
sweet corn

makrill
mahk • rihl
mackerel

mandarin
man • da • reen
tangerine/ mandarin orange

mandel
man • dehl
almond

mandeltårta
man • dehl • toar • ta
almond tart

marmelad
mahr • meh • lahd
marmalade

marsipan
mahr • sih • pahn
marzipan

marulk
mahr • eulk
monkfish

maräng
mah • rehng
meringue

marängsviss
mah • rehng • svihs
meringue served
with cream and
chocolate sauce

matjesill
ma • shcheh • sihl
marinated herring

med citron
meed see • troan
with lemon

med florsocker
meed floar • soh • ker
with icing

med grädde
meed greh • der
with cream

med is
meed ees
with ice

med kolsyra
meed koal • sew • ra
carbonated (drink)

med mjölk
meed myurlk
with milk

med socker
meed soh • kehr
with sugar

med tonic
meed toh • nihk
with tonic water

med vatten
meed va • tehrn
with water

med vitlök
meed veet • lurk
with garlic

medaljong
meh • dal • yong
small fillet of cut
meat

medium
meh • dee • yuhm
medium

mellanmål
meh • lan • moal
snack

(vatten)melon
(va • tehrn)meh • loan
(water)melon

meny
meh • neu
menu

mesost
mees • oast
soft, sweet whey cheese

middag
mih • dahg
dinner

milkshake
milk • shake
milk shake

mineralvatten
mih • neh • rahl • va • tehrn
mineral water

mjuk pepparkaka
myeuk peh • par • kah • ka
soft ginger cake

mjukost
myeuk • oast
soft cheese

mjöl
myurl
flour

mjölk
myurlk
milk

mogen
moa • gehn
ripe

morot
moa • roht
carrot

mousserande
moa • see • ran • der
sparkling (wine)

muffin
muh • fihn
muffin

mullbär
muhl • bair
mulberry

multe
muhl • ter
mullet

munk
muhnk
donut

muskot
muhs • koht
nutmeg

müsli
mews • lee
granola [muesli]

mussla
muhs • la
mussel

mustigt
muhs • tihkt
full-bodied (wine)

mycket kryddad
mew • keht krew • dad
highly seasoned

mycket torrt
mew • keht tohrt
very dry (wine, etc.)

mynta
mewn • ta
mint (herb)

mäktig
mehk • tihg
rich (sauce)

mördegstårta
muhr • deegs • toar • ta
tart (sweet or savory)

mört
murtt
roach (type of fish)

nejlika
nay • lih • ka
clove

nektarin
nehk • ta • reen
nectarine

njure
nyeu • rer
kidney

nudel
neu • dehl
noodle

nyponsoppa
new • pohn • sohp • a
rose-hip soup

nötkött
nurt • churt
red meat

odlade champinjon
_oad • lah • der sham • peen • yoa_n
cultivated mushroom

ojäst bröd
oa • yairst brurd
unleavened bread

oliv
o • leev
olive

olja och vinäger
oal • ya ohk vee • nai • gehr
oil and vinegar

omelett
om • eh • leht
omelet

ost
oast
cheese

ostbricka
oast • brih • ka
cheese plate

ostkaka
oast • kah • ka
curd cake served with jam

ostkex
oast • kehx
cheese cracker

ostron
oa • strohn
oyster

oxkött
oax • churt
ox

oxrullad
oax • reu • lahd
braised roll of beef

oxsvans
oax • svans
oxtail

oxsvanssoppa
oax • svans • sohp • a
oxtail soup

paj
pay
pie

palsternacka
pal • stehr • na • ka
parsnip

pannbiff
pan • bihf
beef patty

pannkaka — pancake
pan • kah • ka

paprika — pepper (fresh)
pah • prih • ka

pasta — pasta
pas • ta

pastarätt — pasta dish
pas • ta • rairt

pastej — pâté
pa • _stay_

peppar — pepper (condiment)
peh • par

pepparkaka — ginger cookie
peh • par • _kah_ • ka

pepparrotssås — horseradish sauce
peh • pa • roat • soas

persika — peach
pair • shih • ka

persilja — parsley
pair • _shihl_ • ya

piggvar — turbot
pihg • vahr

pitabröd — pita bread
pee • ta • brurd

plommon — plum
ploa • mohn

plättar — small pancakes served with jam and whipped cream
pleh • tar

pomegranat äpple — pomegranate
pom • eh • gra • _naht_ • ehp • leh

pommes frites — French fries
pohm • friht

portion — portion
pohrt • _shoan_

portvin
pohrt • veen
port

potatis
poa • tah • tihs
potato

potatismos
poa • tah • tihs • moas
mashed potatoes

potatissoppa
poa • tah • tihs • sohp • a
potato soup

prinsesstårta
prihn • sehs • toar • ta
sponge cake with (vanilla) custard, whipped cream and jam, covered in light green marzipan

prinskorv
prihns • kohrv
small pork sausage

prästost
prehst • oast
hard cheese with a strong, rich flavor

pumpa
puhm • pa
pumpkin

punsch
peunsh
sweet liqueur

purjolök
peur • yoh • lurk
leek

pytt i panna
pewt • ee • pa • na
chunks of fried meat, onion and potatoes

på beställning
poa beh • stehl • nihng
made on request

pärlande
pair • lan • der
sparkling

pärlhöns
pairl • hurns
guinea fowl

päron
pai • rohn
pear

rabarber
rah • bar • behr
rhubarb

ragu
ra • gue
beef stew

rapphöna
rap • hurna
partridge

ren
reen
reindeer

renat
ree • nat
flavorless, clear
spirit (aquavit)

renstek
reen • steek
roast reindeer

revbensspjäll
reev • beens • spehl
spare ribs

riktigt blodig
rihk • tihgt bloa • dihg
very rare

rimmad lax
rih • mad lax
lightly salted
salmon

ris
rees
rice

rocka
roh • ka
ray (type of fish)

rom
rohm
rum

rosé
roh • seh
blush (wine)

rosmarin
roas • ma • reen
rosemary

rostat bröd
rohs • tat brurd
toast

rostbiff
rohst • bihf
roast beef

rova
roa • va
turnip

rumpstek — rump steak
ruhmp • steek

russin — raisin
ruh • sihn

rå — raw
roa

rådjur — venison
roa • yeur

rådjursstek — roast of venison
roa • yeur • steek

rågbröd — rye bread
roag • brurd

rädisa — radish
raid • dih • sa

räkor — shrimp [prawns]
rair • kohr

rätt — dish
reht

röd paprika — sweet red pepper
rurd pah • pree • ka

röd vinbär — red currant
rurd veen • bair

rödbeta — beet
rurd • bee • ta

röding — char
rur • dihng

rödkål — red cabbage
rurd • koal

rödspätta — plaice
rurd • speh • ta

rökt fisk — smoked fish
rurkt fisk

rökt lax — smoked salmon
rurkt lax

rökt renstek *rurkt <u>reen</u> • steek*	smoked reindeer
rökt skinka *rurkt <u>shihng</u> • ka*	smoked ham
rökt ål *rurkt oal*	smoked eel
rörd soppa *rurrd <u>sohp</u> • a*	cream soup
rött *rurt*	red (wine)
sadel *<u>sah</u> • dehl*	saddle (cut of meat)
saffransbullar *<u>sa</u> • frans • buh • lar*	Christmas saffron buns
saft *saft*	squash (fruit cordial)
salamikorv *sa • lah • <u>mee</u> • kohrv*	salami
sallad *<u>sal</u> • ad*	salad
salladshuvud *<u>sal</u> • ads • heu • vuhd*	head of lettuce
salt *salt*	salt
saltade jordnötter *<u>sal</u> • ta • der <u>yoard</u> • nur • ter*	salted peanuts
saltgurka *<u>salt</u> • geur • ka*	salted, pickled gherkin
salvia *sal • <u>vee</u> • a*	sage
sardin *sar • <u>deen</u>*	sardine
schalottenlök *sha • loh • <u>tehn</u> • lurk*	shallot

schnitzel
shniht • sehl
escallope

selleri
seh • leh • ree
celery

senap
see • nap
mustard

sherry
sheh • ree
sherry

sill
sihl
herring

sillbricka
sihl • brih • ka
variety of marinated herring

sillsallad
sihl • sal • ad
beet and herring salad

sirap
seh • rap
syrup

sjömansbiff
shur • mans • bihf
casserole of fried beef, onions and potatoes, braised in beer

sjötunga
sjur • teung • a
sole

skaldjur
skahl • yeur
shellfish

skaldjurssallad
skahl • yeurs • sal • ad
shellfish salad

skarpsill
skarp • sihl
herring

skinka
skihng • ka
ham

skogssvamp
skoags • svamp
field mushroom

sky
shewy
gravy

skåne
skoa • ner

type of aquavit flavored with aniseed and caraway

smultron
smeul • trohn

wild strawberry

småbröd
smoa • brurd

roll

småkaka
smoa • kah • ka

cookie [biscuit]

smårätt
smoa • rairt

snack

småsill
smoa • sihl

herring

smör
smur

butter

smördeg
smur • deeg

pastry

smörgås
smur • goas

Swedish open-faced sandwich

snigel
sneeg • ehl

snail

socker
soh • kehr

sugar

sockerdricka
soh • kehr • drih • ka

lemonade

sockerkaka
soh • kehr • kah • ka

sponge cake

sockerärta
soh • kehr • air • ta

sugar snap pea [mangetout]

sodavatten
soa • da • va • tehrn

soda water

soppa
sohp • a

soup

S.O.S. (smör, ost och sill)
ehs oa ehs (smur oast ohk sihl)

small plate of marinated herring, read, butter and cheese

sparris
spar • ihs

asparagus

sparrissoppa
spa • rihs • sohp • a

asparagus soup

specialitet för landsdelen
speh • sih • ahl • ih • teet furr lands • deel • ehn

local specialty

spenat
speh • naht

spinach

spenatsoppa
speh • naht • sohp • a

spinach soup

sprit
spreet

spirits

spädgris
spaird • grees

unweaned piglet

squash
skoawsh

squash (vegetable)

stark
stark

strong (flavor)

starkt kryddad
starkt krew • dad

hot (spicy)

stek
steek

roast

stekt fisk
steekt fisk

fried fish

stekt kyckling
steekt chewk • lihng

fried chicken (not breaded)

stekt potatis
steekt poa • tah • tihs

sautéed potato

stekt ägg
steekt ehg

fried egg

strömming
strurm • ihng
sprats (small Baltic herring)

strömmingsflundra
strurm • ihngs • fleun • dra
Baltic herring, filleted and sandwiched in pairs, fried, with dill and butter filling

stuvad abborre
steu • vad a • bohr • er
perch poached with onion, parsley and lemon

sufflé
suh • fleh
soufflé

sultana
suhl • tahn • a
sultana raisin

sur
seur
sour

svamp
svamp
mushroom

svart vinbär
svart veen • bair
black currant

svecia
sveh • see • a
semi-hard cheese

svensk punsch
sven • sk peunsh
Swedish punch (sweet liqueur)

sylt
sewlt
jam

sås
soas
sauce

sötningsmedel
surt • nihngs • mee • dehl
artificial sweetener

sötpotatis
surt • poa • tah • tihs
sweet potato

sötsur sås
surt • seur soas
sweet-and-sour sauce

sött	sweet
suht	
T-benstek	T-bone steak
tee • been • steek	
thé	tea
tee	
timjan	thyme
tihm • yan	
toast skagen	toast with chopped shrimp in mayonnaise, topped with bleak roe
toast skah • gehn	
tomat	tomato
toa • maht	
tomater och lök	tomato and onion salad
toa • mah • ter ohk lurk	
tomatjuice	tomato juice
toa • maht • yoas	
tomatsoppa	tomato soup
toa • maht • soh • pa	
tomatsås	tomato sauce
toa • maht • soas	
tonfisk	tuna
toan • fihsk	
tonic	tonic water
toh • nihk	
torkade dadel	dried date
tohr • ka • der dah • dehl	
torkade fikon	dried fig
tohr • ka • der fee • kohn	
torrt	dry
tohrt	
torsk	cod
torshk	

tunga
tuhng • a
tongue (cow)

tunn sås
tuhnn soas
light (sauce)

tunnbröd
tuhnn • brurd
Swedish flat bread, can be soft or crispy

tårta
toarta
sponge-based fruit or cream cake

ugnsbakad fisk
eungns • bah • kad fihsk
oven-baked fish

ugnsstekt kyckling
eungn • steekt chewk • lihng
roast chicken

ugnsstekt potatis
eungn • steekt poa • tah • tihs
roast potato

utan koffein
eu • tan ko • feen
decaffeinated

vaktel
vak • tehl
quail

valfria tillbehör
vahl • free • a tihl • beh • hurr
choice of side dishes

valnöt
vahl • nurt
walnut

vanilj
va • nihly
vanilla

vaniljsås
va • nihly • soas
vanilla sauce, often like custard

varmchoklad
varm shoa • klahd
hot chocolate

varmkorv
varm kohrv
hot dog

varmrätt
varm • rairt
warm meal, usually main course

varmt
varmt
hot

vatten
va • tehrn
water

vattenkrasse
va • tehrn • kra • ser
watercress

vaxböna
vax • bur • na
butter bean

vegetarisk meny
vehg • eh • tah • risk meh • neu
vegetarian menu

vermouth
vehr • meutt
vermouth

vetemjöl
vee • teh • mjurl
wheat flour
(regular)

whisky
vihs • kee
whisky

wienerbröd
vee • nehr • brurd
Danish pastry

wienerschnitzel
vee • nehr • shniht • sehl
breaded veal cutlet

vild champinjon
vihl • da sham • pihn • yoan
wild mushroom

vildand
vihld • and
wild duck

vilt
vihlt
game

viltpastej
vihlt • pa • stay
game pâté

vin
veen
wine

vinaigrettesås
vih • neh • greht • soas
vinaigrette [French
dressing]

vinbär
veen • bair
currant

vindruva
veen • dreu • va
grape

vinlista
veen • lihs • ta

wine list

vispgrädde
visp • greh • der

whipped cream

vit sås
veet soas

white sauce

vitkål
veet • koal

white cabbage

vitkålssallad
veet • koal • sal • ad

coleslaw

vitling
veet • lihng

whiting

vitlök
veet • lurk

garlic

vitlöksmajonnäs
veet • lurks • may • oa • nairs

garlic mayonnaise

vitlökssås
veet • lurk • soas

garlic sauce

vinbär
veen • bair

currant

vindruva
veen • dreu • va

grape

vinlista
veen • lihs • ta

wine list

vispgrädde
visp • greh • der

whipped cream

vitt
viht

white (wine)

vitt bröd
viht brurd

white bread

vodka
vod • ka

vodka

vol au vent
vohl • oa • vahnt

vol-au-vent (pastry filled with meat or fish)

våffla (med sylt och grädde)
vohf • la meed sewlt ohk _greh_ • der
waffle (with jam and whipped cream)

vårlök
voar lurk
shallot [spring onion]

västerbotten
vehs • tehr • boh • tehn
strong, tangy, hard cheese

västkustsallad
vehst • kuhst • _sal_ • ad
west coast salad, with shrimp [prawns] and mussels

yoghurt
yoa • geurt
yogurt

zucchini
seu • _kee_ • nee
zucchini [courgette]

ål
oal
eel

ångkokt fisk
oang • koakt fisk
steamed fish

ädelost
air • dehl • oast
blue cheese

ägg
ehg
egg

äggplanta
ehg • plan • ta
eggplant [aubergine]

äggula
ehg • geu • la
egg yolk

äggröra
ehg • rur • ra
scrambled egg

äggvita
ehg • vee • ta
egg white

älg
ehly
moose

älgfilé
ehly • fih • _leh_
fillet of moose

älgstek	moose roast
ehly • steek	
älgstek med svampsås	roast moose with
ehly • steek meed svamp • soas	mushroom sauce
äppelkaka	apple cake
eh • pehl • kah • ka	
äppelpaj	apple tart
ehp • ehl • pay	
äppelring	apple fritter
ehp • ehl • rihng	
äpple	apple
ehp • leh	
ärta	pea
air • ta	
ärtsoppa	green or yellow pea
airt • sohp • a	soup
ättiksgurka	sweet, pickled
eh • tihks • geur • ka	gherkins
öl	beer
url	
öl på flaska	bottled beer
url poa fla • ska	

PEOPLE

GOING OUT

NEED TO KNOW

Do you have a program of events?	**Har ni ett evenemangsprogram?** *hahr nee eht* *eh • vehn • eh • <u>mangs</u> • proa • gram*
What's playing at the movies [cinema] tonight?	**Vad visas på bio ikväll?** *vahd <u>vee</u> • sas poa <u>bee</u> • oa ee • <u>kvehl</u>*
Where's...?	**Var ligger...?** *vahr <u>lih</u> • gehr...*
the downtown area	**centrum** *<u>sehn</u> • truhm*
the bar	**baren** *<u>bah</u> • rehn*
the dance club	**diskoteket** *dis • koh • <u>tee</u> • keht*

ENTERTAINMENT

Can you recommend...?	**Kan du rekommendera...?** *kan deu reh • koh • mehn • <u>dee</u> • ra...*
a concert	**en konsert** *ehn kohn • <u>sair</u>*
a movie	**en film** *ehn film*
an opera	**en opera** *ehn <u>oa</u> • peh • ra*
a play	**en teaterpjäs** *ehn tee • <u>ah</u> • tehr • pjais*

When does it start/ end?	**När börjar/slutar den?** *nair <u>bur</u> • yar/<u>sleu</u> • tar dehn*
What's the dress code?	**Vilken klädsel gäller?** *<u>vihl</u> • kehn klaid • sehl <u>gehl</u> • lehr*
I like…	**Jag tycker om…** *yahg <u>tew</u> • kehr ohm…*
classical music	**klassisk musik** *<u>klas</u> • isk meu • <u>seek</u>*
folk music	**folkmusik** *<u>folk</u> • meu • <u>seek</u>*
jazz	**jazz** *yas*
pop music	**popmusik** *<u>pop</u> • meu • <u>seek</u>*
rap	**rap** *rap*

For Tickets, see page 45.

YOU MAY HEAR… 💬

| **Stäng av mobiltelefonen, tack.**
stehng afv
mo • <u>beel</u> • teh • leh • <u>foa</u> • nen tak | Turn off your
cell [mobile]
phones, please. |

NIGHTLIFE

What's there to do at night?	**Vad kan man göra på kvällarna?** *vahd kan man yur•ra poa kvehl•ar•na*
Can you recommend...?	**Kan du rekommendera...?** *kan deu reh•koh•mehn•dee•ra...*
a bar	**en bar** *ehn bahr*
a casino	**ett kasino** *eht ka•see•noh*
a dance club	**ett diskotek** *eht dis•koh•tehk*
a gay club	**en gayklubb** *ehn gay•kluhb*
a jazz club	**en jazzklubb** *ehn yas•kluhb*
a club with local music	**en klubb med lokal musik** *ehn kluhb meed lo•kahl meu•seek*
a nightclub	**en nattklubb** *ehn nat•kluhb*
Is there live music?	**Spelar man livemusik där?** *spee•lar man live•meu•seek dair*
How do I get there?	**Hur kan jag komma dit?** *heur kan yahg koh•ma deet*
Is there a cover charge?	**Är det kuvertavgift?** *air de keu•vair•afv•yihft*
Let's go dancing.	**Vi går ut och dansar.** *vee goar eut ohk dan•sar*
Is this area safe at night?	**Är detta område säkert på natten?** *ehr deh•ta ohm•roh•deh seh•kehrt poh na•tehn*

Sweden has produced several world famous pop and rock bands, and music is an important part of contemporary culture and entertainment. The government generously supports independent musicians, as well as smaller music groups, orchestras and symphonies. In larger cities and towns you'll easily find concerts and performances to attend, and information should be listed at the tourist office or its webpage regarding upcoming concerts and events. If you are traveling in Sweden during the summer, attending a music festival is an unforgettable experience. **The Peace & Love Festival** in Borlänge, just two hours from Stockholm, is popular among the younger crowd. Stockholm is home to **Ung08**, which is Europe's largest youth festival, geared toward 13-19 year olds. **The Hultsfred Festival**, in southern Sweden, is the oldest and largest festival. There are also a host of other music festivals covering everything from folk music, to pop and jazz.

ROMANCE

NEED TO KNOW

Would you like to go out for a drink/dinner?	**Har du lust att ta en drink/gå ut och äta?** *hahr deu luhst at tah ehn drihnk/goa eut ohk air•ta*
What are your plans for tonight/tomorrow?	**Vad har du för planer för ikväll/imorgon?** *vahd hahr deu furr plah•nehr furr ee•kvehl/ee•mo•ron*
Can I have your number?	**Kan jag få ditt telefonnummer?** *kan yahg foa diht teh•leh•foan•nuhm•ehr*
May I join you?	**Får jag göra dig sällskap?** *foar yahg yurra dihg sehl•skahp*
Can I buy you a drink?	**Får jag bjuda på en drink?** *foar yahg byeu•da poa ehn drihnk*
I like you.	**Jag gillar dig.** *yahg yihi•ar day*
I love you.	**Jag älskar dig.** *yahg ehl•skar day*

THE DATING GAME

Would you like to…?	**Har du lust att…?** *hahr deu luhst at…*
go out for coffee	**gå ut och ta en kopp kaffe** *goa eut ohk tah ehn kohp ka•fer*

go for a drink	**ta en drink**
	tah ehn drihnk
go out for a meal	**gå ut och äta**
	goa eut ohk air • ta
What are your plans for...?	**Vad har du för planer för...?**
	vahd hahr deu furr plah • nehr furr...
today	**idag**
	ee • dahg
tonight	**ikväll**
	ee • kvehl
tomorrow	**imorgon**
	ee • mo • ron
this weekend	**den här helgen**
	dehn hair hehl • yehn
Where would you like to go?	**Vart vill du gå?**
	vart vihl deu goa
I'd like to go to...	**Jag skulle vilja gå till...**
	yahg skuh • ler vihl • ya goa tihl...
Do you like...?	**Tycker du om...?**
	tew • kehr deu ohm...
Can I have your number/e-mail?	**Kan jag få ditt nummer/din e-post?**
	kan yahg foa diht nuhm • ehr/dihn ee • pohst
Are you on Facebook/ Twitter?	**Finns du på Facebook/Twitter?**
	fihns deu poa Facebook/Twitter
Can I join you?	**Får jag följa med?**
	foar yahg furl • ya meed
You're very attractive.	**Du är väldigt snygg.**
	deu air vehl • dihkt snewgg
You look great!	**Vad du ser vacker ut!**
	vahd deu seer va • kehr eut
Shall we go somewhere quieter?	**Ska vi gå till ett lugnare ställe?**
	skah vee goa tihl eht luhng • na • rer stehl • ler

For Communications, see page 84.

ACCEPTING & REJECTING

Thank you. I'd love to.	**Tack, det vill jag gärna.**
	tak dee vihl yahg <u>yair</u> • na
Where should we meet?	**Var ska vi träffas?**
	vahr skah vee <u>treh</u> • fas
I'll meet you at the bar/your hotel.	**Vi träffas i baren/på ditt hotell.**
	*vee <u>treh</u> • fas ee <u>bahr</u> • en/p**oa** diht hoh • <u>tehl</u>*
I'll come by at...	**Jag kommer...**
	yahg koh • mehr...
What's your address?	**Vilken address har du?**
	Vihl • kehn ahd • rehs hahr deu
Thank you, but I'm busy.	**Tack, men jag är upptagen.**
	tak men yahg air <u>uhp</u> • tah • gehn
I'm not interested.	**Jag är inte intresserad.**
	yahg air <u>in</u> • ter in • treh • <u>see</u> • rad
Leave me alone, please!	**Kan du lämna mig ifred, tack!**
	kan deu <u>lehm</u> • na may ee • <u>freed</u> tak
Stop bothering me!	**Sluta störa mig!**
	<u>sluh</u> • ta <u>stur</u> • ra may

GETTING INTIMATE

Can I hug/kiss you?	**Får jag krama/kysa dig?**
	foar yahg krah•ma/chews•a day
Yes.	**Ja.**
	yah
No.	**Nej.**
	nay
Stop!	**Stopp!**
	stop

SEXUAL PREFERENCES

Are you gay?	**Är du gay?**
	air deu gay
I'm...	**Jag är...**
	yahg air...
heterosexual	**heterosexuell**
	heh•tehr•ro•sehk•shew•ehl
homosexual	**homosexuell**
	hoh•moa•sehk•shew•ehl
bisexual	**bisexuell**
	bee•sehk•shew•ehl
Do you like men/	**Gillar du män/kvinnor?**
women?	*yih•lahr deu mehn/kvih•nohr*

For Grammar, see page 14.

DICTIONARY

ENGLISH–SWEDISH

A

about (approximately) omkring
accept v acceptera
accident olycka
accommodation logi
acetaminophen paracetamol
across över
acupuncture akupunktur
adapter adapter
address n adress
adopt v adoptera
after efter
age ålder
air conditioning
luftkonditionering
air mail flygpost
airline flygbolag
airport flygplats
aisle seat plats i mittgången
all alla
allergic allergisk
allergic reaction allergisk
reaktion
allergy allergi
allow v tillåta
alter v ändra på
alternate route annan väg
aluminum foil aluminiumfolie
a.m. fm
ambulance ambulans
amount summa
amusement park nöjesfält
and och

anemic anemisk
animal djur
another annan
antiques store antikaffär
antiseptic cream antiseptisk
salva
anyone någon
anything något
apartment lägenhet
apologize v be om ursäkt
appliance apparat
approve v godkänna
area code riktnummer
aromatherapy aroma-terapi
arrival ankomst
arrive v anlända
ask v fråga
aspirin huvudvärkstablett
asthma astma
at vid
ATM Bankomat
attack n anfall
audio guide audioguide
authentic äkta
automatic automatisk
available ledig
away iväg

B

baby baby
baby bottle nappflaska
baby formula välling
baby wipes våtservetter för barn

adj adjective	**BE** British English	**v** verb
adv adverb	**n** noun	

babysitter barnvakt
backpack ryggsäck
bad dålig
bag (shopping) påse
baggage cart bagagekärra
baggage claim bagageutlämning
bakery bageri
band (music group) band
bandage (gauze) gasbinda
bank bank
bank charge bankavgift
banknote sedel
bar bar
barber herrfrisör
bath bad
bathroom badrum; **(toilet)** toalett
battery batteri
battlefield slagfält
be v vara
beach strand
beautiful vacker
become v bli
bed n säng
before före
begin v börja
behind bakom
belt skärp
between mellan
big stor
bicycle cykel
bicycle lock cykelås
bikini bikini
bill n **(restaurant bill)** nota;
  (hotel, invoice) räkning
birthday födelsedag
bite n bett; v **(bite)** bita; v **(chew)**
  tugga
black svart
blanket n täcke
bleed v blöda
blood blod
blood pressure blodtryck

blouse blus
board v **(flight)** borda
boarding house pensionat
boarding pass (airport)
  boardingkort
boat båt
boat tour båttur
book bok
bookstore bokhandel
boots stövlar
boring trist
botanical garden botanisk
  trädgård
bottle flaska
bottle opener flasköppnare
bowl djup tallrik
boy pojke
boyfriend pojkvän
bra behå
bracelet armband
break v gå sönder
breakdown v **(car)** gå sönder
breastfeed v amma
breathe andas
bridge bro
bring ta med
broken (broken) sönder;
  (damaged) trasig
brooch brosch
broom sopborste
brown brun
burn v brinna
bus buss
bus route busslinje
bus station bussterminal
bus stop busshållplats
business center businesscenter
business hours öppettider
business trip affärsresa
busy upptagen
but men
buy v köpa

C

cabin stuga
cafe kafé
calender kalender
call v (phone) ringa
calm lugn
camera kamera
camping bed tältsäng
can n burk; v (be able to) kan
can opener konservöppnare
cancel v avbeställa
car bil
car deck (ferry) bildäck
car ferry bilfärja
car park [BE] parkeringsplats
car rental biluthyrning
car seat bilbarnstol
carafe karaff
card n kort
carry on n (luggage) handbagage
cash kontant
cashier (male) kassör; (female)
   kassörska
casino kasino
castle slott
cathedral katedral
cave grotta
cell phone mobiltelefon
ceramics keramik
certificate of authenticity
   äkthetsbevis
chair lift stollift
change n (money) växel; v
   (transportation; a baby) byta; v
   (reservation) ändra;
cheap billig
check in v checka in
check in desk (airport)
   incheckning
check out v checka ut
checking account checkkonto

chemical toilet kemisk toalett
chemist [BE] apotek
chest bröstet
child barn
child's cot [BE] barnsäng
children's menu barnmeny
church kyrka
cigar cigarr
cinema [BE] bio
city (city) stad; (downtown)
   centrum
city map stadskarta
classical music klassiskmusik
clean n ren
cleaning supplies städutrustning
clear v (computer) rensa
cliff klippa
cling film [BE] plastfolie
clock klocka
close v stänga
closed stängt
clothing store klädaffär
coat rock
coffee shop konditori
coin mynt
cold (illness) förskylning;
   (temperature) kall
colleague kollega
color färg
comb kam
come v komma
company (business) firma;
   (companionship) sällskap
computer dator
concert konsert
conditioner hårbalsam
condom kondom
conference konferens
conference room konferensrum
confirm v (reservation) bekräfta
contact lens solution
   kontaktlinsvätska

contain v innehålla

contraceptive preventivmedel

convention hall kongresshall

cooking facilities kokmöjligheter

cool (temperature) sval

copy n kopia

copy machine kopieringsautomat

corkscrew korkskruv

correct rätt

cost v kosta

cotton bomull

cough n hosta; v hosta

country code landsnummer

cover charge kuvertavgift

credit card kreditkort

crib barnsäng

cross country skiing längdåkning

crystal (glass) kristallglas

cup kopp

culture kultur

currency valuta

currency exchange office
  växelkontor

customs tull

customs declaration form
  tulldeklaration

cute adj gullig

cycling cykelåkning

D

dala horse dalahäst

damage v (damage) skada; n
  (harm) skada

dance v dansa

dance club diskotek

day ticket dagsbiljett

day trip dagstur

deaf döv

debit card bankkort

declare v (customs) förtulla

deck chair solstol

deep djup

delay n försening

delete v (computer) radera

delicatessen delikatessaffär

denim denim

dentist tandläkare

denture tandprotes

deodorant deodorant

depart v (train) avgå

department store varuhus

departure (airport) avgång

departure gate avgångsgate

deposit handpenning

desire adj gärna; n lust

detour trafikomläggning

develop v (photos) framkalla

diabetic n diabetiker

dial v (number) slå

diamond diamant

diaper blöja

diarrhea diarré

diesel diesel

difficult svårt

digital digital

digital print digitalt kort

dirty smutsig

disabled rörelsehindrad

disabled accessible toilet [BE]
  handicappanpassad toalett

discount rabatt

discount card rabattkort

dish detergent diskmedel

dishwasher diskmaskin

display case vitrin

disposable camera
  engångskamera

disturb v störa

dive v dyka

divide v dela

diving equipment
  dykarutrustning

divorced skild

dizzy yr

do v (do something) göra; (work with) syssla med
do not disturb var god stör ej
doctor doktor
doll docka
dollar dollar
domestic (travel) inrikes
domestic flight inrikes flyg
domestic partner sambo
door dörr
dosage dosering
downtown centrum
dress klänning
dress code klädsel
drive v köra
driver's license körkort
drops (medication) droppar
dry cleaner kemtvätt
dubbed dubbad
duty free taxfri
duty free good taxfri vara

E

each varje
ear öra
earring örhänge
east öster
easy lätt
eat v äta
economy class turist klass
electrical outlet nätuttag
elevator hiss
e-mail e-post
e-mail address e-postadress
emergency nödsituation
emergency brake nödbroms
emergency exit nödutgång
English engelska
engrave v gravera
enter n (entrance) ingång; (computer) enter
entertainment underhållning

equipment utrustning
escalator rulltrappa
e-ticket e-biljett
European Union (EU) europeiska unionen
event händelse
examine v (medical) undersöka
excess baggage överviktsbagage
exchange rate växelkursen
excuse me (attention, pardon) ursäkta; (to get past) ursäkta mig
exit n (way out) utgång
expensive dyr
expert avancerad
express express
express mail expresspost
extension (phone) anknytning
eyeglasses glasögon

F

fabric tyg
family familj
fan (ventilation) fläkt
fantastic adj fantastisk
fare biljettpris
farm bondgård
fast fort
fax fax
fax machine fax machine
female kvinna
ferry färja
fever feber
field fält
fill v (prescription) göra i ordning
filling (dental) plomb
film [BE] film
fire exit brandutgång
first första
fishing fiske
fit v (clothing) passa
fitting room provrum

fix v laga
fixed price fast pris
flat [BE] lägenhet
flight flyg
flight number flygnummer
floor (level) våning
football [BE] fotboll
for (someone) för
foreign currency utländsk valuta
forest skog
forget v glömma
fork gaffel
form n blankett
fountain fontän
free (available) ledig
free of charge gratis
freezer frys
friend vän
from ifrån
frying pan stekpanna
fun rolig
function v (work) fungera
further (more) ytterligare

G

game spel
garbage sopor
garbage bag soppåse
gasoline bensin
gas station bensinstation
gate (boarding) gate
genuine äkta
get off (train) stiga av
gift shop presentaffär
gift present
girlfriend flickvän
give v ge
glass (drinking) glas
gold guld
golf golf
golf club golfklubba
golf course golfbana

good adj bra
goodbye hej då
greengrocer [BE] livsmedelsaffär
grocery store livsmedelsaffär
group grupp
guest gäst
guide (brochure) guide; (person) guide
guide dog ledarhund
gym gym

H

hair cut klippning
hair dryer hårtork
hair style frisyr
hairbrush hårborste
hairdresser damfrisör
hairspray hårspray
half halv
handbag [BE] handväska
handicapped rörelsehindrade
handicapped accessible toilet handicappanpassad toalett
handicraft hantverk
handmade handgjord
hat hatt
have v ha
health food store hälsokostaffär
hearing impaired hörselskadad
heat värme
helmet hjälm
help n hjälp; v hjälpa
here här
hi hej
highchair barnstol
highway motorväg
hike v vandra
hiking vandring
hill kulle
hire v [BE] rent
holiday [BE] (vacation) semester
holiday (celebration) helgdag

horseback riding ridsport
hospital sjukhus
hot varm
hotel hotell
hour timme
husband man

I

ibuprofen ibuprofen
ice hockey ishockey
identification (idenitification) legitimation; **(ID card)** ID-kort
ill [BE] sjuk
in i
included (in the price) inkluderad
indoor pool inomhusbassäng
information desk information
innocent oskyldig
insect insekt
insect bite insektbett
insect repellent mygg olja
inside inuti
instant messenger instant messenger
instructor instruktör
insurance försäkring
interesting intressant
international (travel) utrikes
international driver's license internationellt körkort
internet internet
internet cafe internetkafé
interpreter tolk
iron *n* **(clothes)** strykjärn; *v* **(clothes)** stryka
itemized bill specificerad räkning

J

jacket jacka
jeans jeans
jet ski jetski
jeweler juvelerare
jewelry smycken

job jobb

K

keep *v* behålla
key nyckel
key card nyckelkort
kiddie pool barnbassäng
kiss *v* kyssa
kitchen kök
knife kniv
krona (Swedish currency) krona

L

lace spets
lactose intolerant laktosinterant
ladies' restroom damtoilett
ladieswear damkläder
lake sjö
last sista
late sen
launderette [BE] snabbtvätt
laundromat snabbtvätt
laundry tvätt
laundry detergent tvättmedel
laundry facilities tvättmöjligheter
lawyer advokat
leather läder
leave *v* lämna
left (direction) vänster
lesson lektion
letter brev
library bibliotek
life boat livbåt
life jacket flytväst
lifeguard livräddare
lift (ski) lift
lift [BE] *n* **(elevator)** hiss
lift pass liftkort
light (lamp) lampa
light bulb glödlampa
lighter tändare
like *v* gilla

line (bus) linje
linen linne
live v bo
loafers loafers
lock v låsa
log on logga in
log out logga ut
long adj lång; adv länge
lose v (lost luggage) förlora; v (drop, lose) tappa
lost n vilse
lost property office [BE] hittegodsexpedition
lost and found hittegodsexpedition
lottery lotto
love v älska
luggage locker förvaringsskåp

M

mail post
mailbox postlåda
manager chef
manicure manikyr
many många
map karta
market marknad
married gift
mass mässan
match (fire) tändsticka
meal måltid
mean v (signify) betyda
measuring spoon måttsked
medicine medicin
medium medium
meet v träffa
meeting sammanträde
memory card minneskort
men's restroom herrtoalett
menstrual cramps mensvärk
menstruation mens
menswear herrkläder

menu meny
message meddelande
microwave mikrovågsugn
minimum minimum
Miss fröken
mistake misstag
mobile phone [BE] mobiltelefon
moment ögonblick
mop n skurmop
moped moped
mosque moské
motel motell
motion sickness åksjuka
motorboat motorbåt
motorcycle motocykel
motorway [BE] motorväg
mountain berg
mouth mun
movie film
movies bio
Mr. herr
Mrs. fru
mugging överfall
multi-day card flerdagskort
museum museum
must måste

N

nail file nagelfil
nail salon nagelvårdssalong
name n namn
napkin servett
nappy [BE] blöja
nature reserve naturreservat
nearby nära
necklace halsband
need v behöva
new ny
newspaper tidning
newsstand tidningskiosk
next nästa
next to bredvid

nice *adj* snäll
no (not allowed) ej
nobody ingen
no smoking rökning förbjuden
north norr
not inte
not included (in the price) inte
  inkluderad
nothing inget
number nummer
nurse sjuksköterska

O

off av
old gammal
on (switch) på
one way (street) enkelriktad
one-way ticket enkel biljett
only bara
open *n* öppet; *v* öppna
opening hours [BE] öppettider
opera opera
opposite mitt emot
optician optiker
or eller
orchestra orkester
order *v* beställa
other andra
outdoor utomhus
outdoor pool utomhusbassäng
outside ute
overnight delivery (mail)
  expressutdelning
oxygen treatment
  syrebehandling

P

pacifier napp
package paket
paddling pool [BE] barnbassäng
pajamas pyjamas
panorama panorama

pants byxor
panty hose strumpbyxor
paper napkin papperservett
parcel [BE] paket
park *n* park; *v* parkera
parking parkering
parking lot parkeringsplats
passport pass
passport control passkontroll
password (computer) lösenord
pay phone telefonautomat
pay *v* betala
peak (mountain) top
pearl pärla
pedestrian crossing
  övergångsställe för fotgängare
pedestrian fotgängare
pedicure pedikyr
pen kulspetspenna
per per
per day per dag
per week per vecka
performance (music, theater)
  föreställning
person person
petite petit
petrol [BE] bensin
petrol station [BE] bensinstation
pewter tenn
pharmacy apotek
phone call samtal
phone card telefonkort
phone number telefonnummer
photo foto
pick up *v* (person/thing) hämta
picnic area picknickområde
piece bit
pill tablett
pillow kudde
PIN PIN kod
pink rosa
piste [BE] spår

place *n* ställe
plan *n* plan
plaster [BE] plåster
plastic wrap plastfolie
platform (train) plattform
platinum platina
plate tallrik
play *n* (theater) teaterpjäs;*v* spela
playground lekplats
playpen lekrum
pleasant trevlig
please (request) snälla;
  (invitation) varsågod
plunger vaskrensare
pocket *n* ficka
point of interest sevärdhet
police polis
police report polisrapport
police station polisstation
pond damm
post office postkontor
postage porto
postcard vykort
pot (cooking pot) gryta;
  (saucepan) kastrull
pound sterling engelsk pund
pregnant gravid
premium (gas) premium
prescription recept
price pris
print (computer) skriva ut
private privat
private room privatrum
problem problem
produce store matbutik
program (events) program
pub pub
public transportation allmänna
  kommunikationer
pull dra
purple lila
purpose syfte

purse (large) handväska, (small)
  portmonnä
push tryck
pushchair [BE] sittvagn

R

racket (tennis) racket
railroad järnväg
railway [BE] järnväg
rain regn
raincoat regnkappa
rap rap
rape *n* våldtäkt
rapids fors
rash *n* utslag
(disposable) razor (engångs)
  rakhyvel
reach *v* nå
read *v* läsa
ready färdig
receipt kvitto
receive *v* ta emot
receptionist receptionist
recommend *v* rekommendera
refrigderator kylskåp
region region
regular gas vanlig
relationship (romantic)
  förhållande
rent *n* hyra; *v* hyra
repair *v* reparera
repairs (car) reparationer
repeat *v* upprepa
report *v* (crime) anmäla
reservation bokning
reserved reserverad
rest area rastplats
restroom (sign) WC
restaurant restaurang
return *v* (give back) återlämna
return ticket [BE] retur (biljett)

reverse charge call [BE] ba-samtal

right (correct) rätt; (direction) höger

ring (jewelry) ring

river flod

road väg

road map vägkarta

romantic romantisk

room rum

room service rumservice

round n (golf) runda

round-trip ticket retur biljett

rubbish [BE] sopor

S

safe n kassaskåp

sailing segling

sandals sandaler

sanitary napkin binda

saucepan kastrull

sauna bastu

save v (collect) spara

scarf halsduk

schedule tidsschema

scissors sax

sea hav

seat (on train) plats

seat number platsnummer

seat reservation (train) sittplatsbiljett

seminar seminarium

send v skicka

separated (couple) separerad

service serveringsavgift

service charge (bank) expeditionsavgift

sex sex

shampoo shampoo

sheet lakan

shoe store skoaffär

shoes skor

shopping basket shoppingkorg

shopping cart shoppingvagn

shopping centre [BE] shoppingcenter

shopping mall shoppingcenter

shorts shorts

show v visa

shower dusch

sick sjuk

side effect biverkning

sightseeing tour sightseeingtur

sign v undertäckna

silk siden

SIM card (cell phone) SIM kort

single ticket [BE] enkel (biljett)

sit v sitta

size storlek

skiing skidåkning

skirt kjol

slice n skiva

slippers tofflor

slippery (icy) hal

slow adj långsam

small liten

sneakers träningsskor

snorkeling equipment snorkelutrustning

snow snö

snowboard snowboard

snowshoes pjäxor

soap tvål

soccer fotboll

sock socka

something något

soon snart

soother [BE] napp

sore throat halsont

sorry förlåt

south söder

souvenir souvenir

spa spa

spatula stekspade

speak *v* tala
spoon sked
sports massage
  träningsmassage
spouse (female) maka; (male)
  make
sprain stukning
square (town feature) torg
stadium stadion
stair trappa
stamp *n* frimärke
stamp your ticket stämpla er
  biljett
start *v* (car) starta
stay *n* stanna
steakhouse stekhus
steep brant
stolen stulen
stomach magen
stomachache ont i magen
stop *n* (bus stop) bushållplats;
  v stanna
store *n* butik; *v* förvara
strange konstig
stream å
street gata
stroller sittvagn
student studerande
study *v* läsa
stunning jättesnygg
subtitle text
suburb förort
subway tunnelbana
subway station
  tunnelbanestation
suitable lämplig
suitcase resväska
sunburn solbränna
sunglasses solglasögon
sunstroke solsting
super [BE] (gas) premium
supermarket snabbköp

surfboard surfbräda
sweater tröja
sweatshirt sweatshirt
Swedish *adj* svensk; (language)
  svenska
swelling svullnad
swim *v* simma
swimming pool simbassäng
swimming trunks badbyxor
swimsuit baddräkt
symbol (computer) tecken
symphony (orchestra) symfoni
synagogue synagoga

T

table bord
tablecloth duk
take *v* ta
take out *v* ta ut
taken (occupied) upptagen
tampon tampong
tax skatt
taxi taxi
teaspoon tesked
temperature temperatur
temple tempel
tennis tennis
tennis court tennisbana
terminal (airport) terminal
terrible förskräcklig
text message sms
textiles textil
thank you tack
theft rån
thief tjuv
think *v* tänka
ticket biljett
ticket machine biljettautomat
ticket office biljettkontor
tie *n* slips
tights [BE] strumpbyxor
timetable [BE] tidsschema

tip (service) dricks
tissue näsduk
to till
tobacconist tobaksaffär
toilet [BE] toalett; (sign) WC
toilet paper toalettpapper
tooth tand
toothbrush tandborste
toothpaste tandkräm
tour tur
tourist turist
tourist attraction turistattraktion
tourist information
  turistinformation
tourist office turistbyrå
town hall stadshus
toy store leksaksaffär
track (railroad) spår
trail spår
train n tåg
train station järnvägsstation
tram spårvagn
translate v översätta
travel v (travel) resa; (drive) åka
travel agency resebyrå
travel agent (female)
  resebyråkvinna; (male)
  resebyråman
travel sickness [BE] åksjuka
traveler's check resecheck
traveller's cheque [BE]
  resecheck
treat v (to a meal) bjuda
trim (hair) putsning
trip n resa
trolley [BE] bagagekärra
trouser [BE] byxor
try v prova
turn off v stänga av
turn on v sätta på

U

ugly ful
umbrella (standard) paraply;
  (sun) solparasol
underground [BE] tunnelbana
underground station [BE]
  tunnelbanestation
understand v förstå
underwear (general) underkläder
unfortunately tyvärr
United Kingdom Storbritanien
unlimited (mileage) obegränsad
until tills
urgent brådskande
United State Förenta Staterna
use v använda
username användarnamn
utensil bestick

V

vacancy ledigt rum
vacation semester
vacuum cleaner dammsugare
vaginal infection vaginal
  infektion
valley dal
valuable värdesak
value n värde
vegetarian vegetarian
viewpoint utsiktspunkt
village by
visit n besök; v besöka
visiting hours besökstid
visitor besökare
visitor besökare
visually impaired syn skadad
vomit v kräkas

W

wait vänta
wake up v vakna

wake-up call telefonväckning
walk n promenad; v gå
wallet plånbok
want v vilja
washing machine tvättmaskin
waterfall vattenfall
weather forecast
   väderleksrapport
weekend helg
welcome välkommen
west väster
wheelchair rullstol
wheelchair ramp rullstolsramp
when när
where var
which vilken
white vitt
who vem
widow änka
widower änkling
window fönster

window seat fönsterplats
windsurfing vindsurfa
wireless internet trådlös internet
with med
withdrawal (bank) uttag
wood trä
wool ull
work from home v arbeta
   hemifrån
wrap v (present) slå in
write v skriva
wrong fel

Y

yellow gul
yes ja
yield lämna företräde
youth hostel vandrarhem

Z

zoo djurpark

SWEDISH–ENGLISH

A

acceptera v accept
adapter adapter
adoptera v adopt
adress n address
advokat lawyer
affärscentrum shopping mall
   [centre BE]
affärsresa business trip
akupunktur acupuncture
alla all
allergi allergy
allergisk allergic
allergisk reaktion allergic
   reaction

allmänna
kommunikationer public
   transportation
alternativ väg alternate route
aluminiumfolie aluminum foil
ambulans ambulance
amma v breastfeed
andas breathe
andra other
anemisk anemic
anfall n attack
anknytning extension (phone)
ankomst arrival
anlända v arrive
anmäla v report (crime)

annan another
antikaffär antiques store
antiseptisk salva antiseptic cream
använda v use
användarnamn username
apotek pharmacy [chemist BE]
apparat appliance
arbeta hemifrån v work from home
armband bracelet
aroma-terapi aromatherapy
astma asthma
audioguide audio guide
automatisk automatic
av off
avancerad expert
avbeställa v cancel
avgå v depart (plane)
avgång departure
avgångsgate departure gate

B

baby baby
bad bath
badbyxor swim trunks
baddräkt swim suit
badrum bathroom [toilet BE]
bagagekärra baggage cart [trolley BE]
bagageutlämning baggage claim
bageri bakery
bakom behind
band band (music group)
bank bank
bankavgift bank charge
bankkort debit card
Bankomat ATM
bar bar
bara only (just)
barn child

barnbassäng kiddie pool [paddling pool BE]
barnmeny children's menu
barnstol highchair
barnsäng crib [child's cot BE]
barnvakt babysitter
bastu sauna
batteri battery
be om ursäkt v apologize
behå bra
behålla v keep
behöva v need
bekräfta v confirm (reservation)
bensin gasoline [petrol BE]
bensinstation gas station [petrol station BE]
berg mountain
bergklättring rock climbing
bestick utensil
beställa v order
besök n visit
besöka v visit
besökare visitor
besökstid visiting hours
betala v pay
bett n bite
betyda mean (signify)
bibliotek library
bikini bikini
bil car
bilbarnstol car seat
bildäck car deck (ferry)
bilfärja car ferry
biljett ticket
biljettautomat ticket machine
biljettkontor ticket office
biljettpris fare
billig cheap
bilsäte car seat
biluthyrning car rental
binda sanitary napkin [towel BE]
bio movies [cinema BE]

bit piece
bita v bite
biverkning side effect
bjuda v treat (to a meal)
blankett n form
bli v become
blod blood
blodtryck blood pressure
blus blouse
blöda bleed
blöja diaper [nappy BE]
bo v live
boardingkort boarding pass
bok book
bokhandel bookstore
bokning reservation (travel, restaurant)
bomull cotton
bondgård farm
bord table
borda v board (flight)
botanisk trädgård botanical garden
bra adj good
brandutgång fire exit
brant steep
bredvid next to
brev letter
brinna v burn
bro bridge
brosch brooch
brun brown
brådskande urgent
bröstet chest
burk n can
businesscenter business center
buss bus
busshållplats bus stop [request stop BE]
busslinje bus route
bussterminal bus station
butik n store

by village
byta v change (baby, connection)
byxor pants [trouser BE]
båt boat
båttur boat tour
börja v begin

C

centrum downtown
checka in check in (airport)
checka ut check out (hotel)
chef manager
cigarr cigar
cykel bicycle
cykelåkning cycling
cykelås bicycle lock

D

dagsbiljett day ticket
dagstur day trip
dal valley
dalahäst dala horse
damfrisör hairdresser
damkläder ladieswear
damtoalett ladies' restroom
damm pond
dammsugare vacuum cleaner
dansa v dance
dator computer
dela divide
delikatessaffär delicatessen
denim denim
deodorant deodorant
diabetiker n diabetic
diamant diamond
diarré diarrhea
diesel diesel
digital digital
digitalt kort digital print
diskmedel dish detergent
diskmaskin dishwasher
djup deep

djup tallrik bowl
djur animal
djurpark zoo
docka doll
doktor doctor
dollar dollar
dosering dosage
dra pull
dricks tip (service)
droppar drops (medication)
dubbad dubbed
duk table cloth
dusch shower
dyka v dive
dykarutrustning diving equipment
dyr expensive
dålig bad
dörr door
döv deaf

E

e-biljett e-ticket
efter after
ej no (do not...)
eller or
endast only (nothing but)
engelska English
engelsk pund pound sterling
engångskamera disposable camera
enkel biljett one-way trip [single ticket BE]
enkelriktad one way (street)
enter enter (computer)
e-post e-mail
e-postadress e-mail address
europeiska unionen European Union (EU)
expeditionsavgift service charge (bank)
express express

expresspost express mail
expressutdelning overnight delivery (mail)

F

familj family
fantastisk adj fantastic
fast pris fixed price
fax fax
fax machine fax machine
feber fever
fel wrong
ficka n pocket
film movie [film BE]
fiske fishing
flaska bottle
flasköppnare bottle opener
flerdagskort multi-day card
flickvän girlfriend
flod river
flyg flight
flygbolag airline
flygnummer flightnumber
flygplats airport
flygpost airmail
fläkt fan
fm a.m.
fontän fountain
fors rapids
fort fast
fotboll soccer [football BE]
fotgängare pedestrian
foto photo
framkalla v develop (photos)
fri free
frimärken stamps
frisyr hair style
fru Mrs.
frys freezer
fråga ask
från from...
fröken Miss

ful ugly
fungera v function (work)
fylla v fill
fält field
färdig ready
färg color
färja ferry
födelsedag birthday
fönster window
fönsterplats window seat
för tung/stor too much, excess (baggage)
före before
Förenta Staterna United States
föreställning performance (music, theater)
förhållande relationship (romantic)
förlora v lose
förlåt sorry
försening n delay
förskräcklig terrible
förskylning cold (sick)
första first
förstå v understand
försäkring insurance
förtulla v declare (customs)
förvaringsskåp luggage locker
förort suburb

G

gaffel fork
gammal adj old, n age
gasbinda bandage (gauze)
gata street
gate gate (boarding)
ge v give
gift married
gilla v like
glas glass (drinking)
glasögon eyeglasses
glödlampa light bulb

glömma v forget
godkänna v approve
golf golf
golfbana golf course
golfklubb golf club
gratis free of charge
gravera v engrave
gravid pregnant
grotta cave
grupp group
gryta pot (cooking)
guide guide (brochure); guide (person)
gul yellow
guld gold
gullig adj cute
gym gym
gå v walk, leave
gå sönder break; breakdown (car)
gärna adj desire
göra v do

H

ha v have
hal slippery (icy)
halsband necklace
halsduk scarf
halsont sore throat
halv halv
handbagage carry on
handgjord handmade
handicappanpassad toalett handicapped accessible toilet [disabled BE]
handpenning deposit
handväska purse [hand bag BE]
hantverk handicraft
hatt hat
hav sea
hej hi
hej då goodbye
helg weekend

helgdag holiday (celebration)
hemifrån work from home
hemlagad homemade (food)
herr Mr.
herrfrisör barber
herrkläder menswear
herrtoalett men's restroom
iss elevator [lift BE]
hittegodsexpedition lost-and-found [lost property office BE]
hjälm helmet
hjälp *n* help
hjälpa *v* help
hosta *n* cough; *v* to cough
hotell hotel
huvudvärkstablett aspirin
hyra rent [hire BE]
hårbalsam conditioner
hårborste hairbrush
hårspray hairspray
hårtork hair dryer
hälsokostaffär health food store
hämta *v* pick up (thing/person)
händelse event
här here
höger right (direction)
hörselskadad hearing impaired

I

i in
ibuprofen ibuprofen
ID-kort identification
ifrån from
incheckning check in desk (airport)
information information desk
ingen nobody (sg)
inget nothing
ingång entrance
inkluderad included (in the price)
innehålla contain

inomhusbassäng indoor swimming pool
inrikes domestic (travel)
inrikes flyg domestic flight
insekt insect
insektbett insect bite
instant messenger instant messenger
instruktör instructor
inte not
inte inkluderad not included (in the price)
internationellt körkort international driver's license
internet internet
internetkafé internet café
intressant interesting
inuti inside
ishockey ice hockey
iväg away

J

ja yes
jacka jacket
jeans jeans
jetski jet ski
jobb job
juvelerare jeweler
järnväg railroad [railway BE]
järnvägsstation train station
jättesnygg stunning

K

kafé café
kalender calendar
kall cold (temperature)
kam comb
kamera camera
kan *v* can (be able to)
karaff carafe
karta map

kasino casino
kassaskåp n safe
kassör cashier (male)
kassörska cashier (female)
kastrull saucepan (cooking)
katedral cathedral
kemisk toalett chemical toilet
kemtvätt dry cleaner
keramik ceramics
kjol skirt
klassiskmusik classical music
klippa cliff
klippning hair cut
klocka(n) clock
klädaffär clothing store
klädsel dress code
klänning dress
kniv knife
kokmöjligheter cooking facilities
kollega colleague
komma v come
konditori coffee shop
kondom condom
konferens conference
konferensrum conference room
kongresshall convention hall
konsert concert
konservöppnare can opener
konstig strange
kontaktlinsvätska contact lens solution
kontant n cash
kopia n copy
kopieringsautomat copy machine
kopp cup
korkskruv corkscrew
kort n card, adj short
kosta v cost
kostym suit (jacket/pants)
kreditkort credit card
kristallglas crystal (glass)

krona krona (Swedish currency)
kräkas v vomit
kudde pillow
kulle hill
kulspetspenna pen
kultur culture
kuvertavgift cover charge
kvinna female
kvitto receipt
kylskåp refridgerator
kyrka church
kyssa v kiss
kök kitchen
köpa v buy
köra drive
körkort driver's license

L

laga v fix
lakan sheet
laktosintolerant lactose intolerant
lampa light (lamp)
landsnummer country code
ledarhund guide dog
ledig available
ledigt rum vacancy
legitimation identification
lekplats playground
lekrum playpen
leksaksaffär toy store
lektion lesson
liftkort liftpass
lila purple
linje line
linne linen
liten small
livbåt life boat
livräddare lifeguard
livsmedelsaffär grocery store [greengrocer BE]
loafers loafers

logga in log on (connect to internet)
logga ut log out
logi accommodation
lotto lottery
luftkonditionering air conditioning
lugn calm
lust n desire
lyft lift (ski)
lång long
långsam slow
låsa v lock
läder leather
lägenhet apartment [flat BE]
lämna v leave
lämna före träde yield
lämplig suitable
längdåkning cross country skiing
länge long (time)
läsa v (book) read; (school) study
lätt easy
lösenord password

M

magen stomach
maka spouse (female)
make spouse (male)
man husband, man
manikyr manicure
marknad market
matbutik produce store (general store) [grocer BE]
med with
meddelande message
medicin medicine
medium medium
mellan between
men but
mens menstruation
mensvärk menstrual cramps
meny menu

mikrovågsugn microwave
minimum minimum (requirement)
minneskort memory card
misstag mistake
mitt emot opposite
mobiltelefon cell phone [mobile phone BE]
moms sales tax [VAT BE]
moped moped
moské mosque
motel motel
motorcykel motorcycle
motorbåt motorboat
motorväg highway [motorway BE]
mun mouth
museum museum
mygg olja insect repellent
mynt coin
måltid meal
många many
måste must
måttsked measuring spoon
mässan mass (catholic)

N

nagelfil nail file
nagelvårdssalong nail salon
namn n name
napp pacifier [soother BE]
nappflaska baby bottle
naturreservat nature reserve
norr north
nota bill (restaurant)
nummer number
ny new
nyckel key
nyckelkort key card
nå v reach
någon anyone
något anything, something
när when
nära nearby

näsduk tissue
nästa next
nätuttag electrical outlet
nödbroms emergency brake
nödsituation emergency
nödutgång emergency exit
nöjesfält amusement park

O

obegränsad unlimited (mileage)
och and
olycka accident
omkring about (approximately)
ont i magen stomachache
opera opera
optiker optician
orkester orchestra

P

paket package [parcel BE]
panorama panorama
papperservett paper napkin
paracetamol acetaminophen
paraply umbrella
park park
parkering parking
parkering på gatan street parking
parkeringsplats (one or several) parking lot [car park BE]
pass passport
passa v fit
passkontroll passport control
pedikyr pedicure
pensionat boarding house
per per
per dag per day
per vecka per week
person person
petit petite
picknickområde picnic area
PIN kod PIN code

pjäxor snowshoes
plan n plan
plastfolie plastic wrap [cling film BE]
platina platinum
plats seat (on train)
plats i mittgången aisle seat
platsnummer seat number
plattform platform (train)
plomb filling
plånbok wallet
pojke boy
pojkvän boyfriend
polis police
polisrapport police report
polisstation police station
porto postage
post mail
postkontor post office
postlåda mail box
premium premium [super BE] (gas)
presentaffär gift shop
present gift
preventivmedel contraceptive
pris price
privat private
privatrum private room
problem problem
program progam (events)
prova v try
provrum fitting room
pub pub
putsning trim (hair)
pyjamas pajamas
på on (switch)
påse bag
pärla pearl

R

rabatt discount
rabattkort discount card

racket racket (tennis)
radera delete (computer)
(engångs)rakhyvel (disposable) razor
rap rap
rastplats rest area
recept prescription
receptionist receptionist
region region
regn rain
regnkappa raincoat
rekommendera v recommend
ren adj clean
rensa clear (computer, ATM), clean
reparationer repairs (car)
reparera v repair
resa v travel, n trip
resebyrå travel agency
resebyråkvinna travel agent (female)
resebyråman travel agent (male)
resecheck traveler's check [traveller's cheque BE]
reserverad reserved
restaurang restaurant
resväska suitcase
retur (biljett) round-trip ticket [return ticket BE]
ridsport horseback riding
riktnummer area code
ring ring (jewelry)
ringa v call (phone)
rock coat
rolig fun
romantisk romantic
rosa pink
rullstol wheelchair
rullstolsramp wheelchair ramp
rulltrappa escalator
rum room
rumservice room service

runda v round (golf)
ryggsäck backpack
rån theft
räkning bill (hotel, invoice)
rätt correct
rökning förbjuden no smoking
rörelsehindrad disabled

S

sambo domestic partner
sammanträde meeting
samtal phone call
sandaler sandals
sax scissors
sedel banknote
segling sailing
semester vacation
seminarium seminar
sen late
separerad separated (couple)
serveringsavgift service
servett napkin
sevärdhet point of interest
sex sex
shampoo shampoo
shoppingcenter shopping mall [shopping centre BE]
shoppingkorg shopping basket
shoppingvagn shopping cart
shorts shorts
siden silk
sightseeingtur sightseeing tour
simbassäng swimming pool
SIM kort SIM card (cell phone)
simma v swim
sista last
sitta v sit
sittplatsbiljett seat reservation (train)
sittvagn stroller [pushchair BE]
sjuk sick [ill BE]
sjukhus hospital

sjuksköterska nurse

sjö lake

skada *n* damage, *v* harm

skatt tax

sked spoon

skicka *v* send

skidåkning skiing

skild divorced

skiva *n* slice

skoaffär shoe store

skog forest

skor shoes

skriva write

skriva ut print

skurmop *n* mop

skyldig innocent

skärp belt

slagfält battlefield

slips tie

slott castle

slå *v* (phone number) dial

slå in *v* wrap (present)

sms text message

smutsig dirty

smycken jewelry

snabbköp supermarket

snabbtvätt Laundromat [launderette BE]

snart soon

snorkelutrustning snorkeling equipment

snowboard snowboard

snäll *adj* nice

snälla (request) please

snö snow

socka sock

solbränna sunburn

solglasögon sunglasses

solsting sunstroke

solstol deck chair

sopborste broom

sopor garbage (garbage disposal) [rubbish BE]

soppåse garbage bag

souvenir souvenir

spa spa

spara *v* save

specifierad räkning itemized bill

spel game

spela *v* play

spets lace

spår trail [piste BE]; track (railroad)

spårvagn tram

stad city

stadion stadium

stadshus town hall

stadskarta city map

stanna *n* stay; *v* stop

starta *v* start

stekhus steakhouse

stekpanna frying pan

stekspade spatula

stiga av get off (train)

stollift chair lift

stor big

Storbritannien United Kingdom

storlek size

strand beach

strumpbyxor panty hose [tights BE]

strykjärn iron (clothes)

studerande student

stuga cabin

stukning *n* sprain

stulen stolen

städutrustning cleaning supplies

ställe place

stämpla er biljett stamp your ticket

stäng av turn off

stänga *v* close

stängt closed

störa disturb

stövlar boots
summa amount
surfbräda surfboard
sval cool (temperature)
svart black
sweatshirt sweatshirt
svensk *adj* swedish
svenska *adj* swedish; (language) Swedish
svullnad swelling
svårt difficult
syfte purpose
symfoni symphony (orchestra)
syn skadad visually impaired
synagoga synagogue
syrebehandling oxygen treatment
syssla med *v* do (work with)
sällskap company (companionship)
säng bed
sätta på turn on
söder south
sönder broken

T

ta *v* take
ta emot *v* receive
ta med bring
ta ut take out
tablett pill (tablet)
tack thank you
tala *v* speak
tallrik plate
tampong tampon
tand tooth
tandborste toothbrush
tandkräm toothpaste
tandläkare dentist
tandprotes dentures
tappa *v* lose; drop
taxfri duty free
taxfri vara duty free good

taxi taxi
teaterpjäs play (theater)
tecken symbol (computer)
telefon katalog telephone catalog
telefonautomat pay phone
telefonkort phone card
telefonnummer phone number
telefonväckning wake up call
temperatur temperature
tempel temple
tenn pewter
tennis tennis
tennisbana tennis court
terminal terminal (airport)
tesked teaspoon
text subtitle
textil textiles
tidning newspaper
tidningskiosk newsstand
tidsschema schedule [timetable BE]
till to
tills until
tillåta *v* allow
timme hour
toalett bathroom [toilet BE]
toalettpapper toilet paper
tobaksaffär tobacconist
tofflor slippers
tolk interpreter
top peak (moutain)
torg square (town feature)
trappa stair
trasig broken (damaged)
trevlig pleasant
trist boring
tryck push
trådlös internet wireless internet
trä wood
träffa *v* meet
träfigur wood carvings

träkniv wooden knife
träningsmassage sports massage
träningsskor sneakers
träsked wooden spoon
träskor wooden clogs
tröja sweater
tugga v chew
tull customs
tulldeklaration customs declaration form
tunnelbana subway [underground BE]
tunnelbanestation subway station [underground station BE]
tur tour
turist tourist
turist klass economy class
turistattraktion tourist attraction
turistbyrå tourist office
turistinformation tourist information
tvål soap
tvätt laundry
tvättmaskin washing machine
tvättmedel laundry detergent
tvättmöjligheter laundry facilities
tyg fabric
tyvärr unfortunately
tåg train
täcke n blanket
tältsäng camping bed
tändare lighter
tändsticka match (fire)
tänka v think

U

ull wool
underhållning entertainment
underkläder underwear (general)
undersöka v examine (medical)
undertäckna v sign

upprepa v repeat
upptagen busy
ursäkta v excuse me (to get attention, pardon me)
ursäkta mig excuse me (to get past)
ute outside
utgång exit way out
utländsk valuta foreign currency
utomhus outdoor
utomhusbassäng outdoor pool
utrikes international (travel)
utrustning equipment
utsiktspunkt view point
utslag n rash
uttag withdrawal (bank)

V

vacker beautiful
vaginal infektion vaginal infection
vakna v wake up
valuta currency
vandra v hike
vandrarhem youth hostel
vandring hiking
vanlig regular gas
var where
var god stör ej do not disturb
vara v be
varje each
varm hot
varsågod (invitation) please
varuhus department store
vaskrensare plunger
vattenfall waterfall
WC (sign) restroom [toilet BE]
veckotidning magazine
vegetarian vegetarian
vem who
vid at
vilja v want

vilken which
vilse lost
visa *v* show
vitrin display case
vitt white
vykort postcard
våldtäkt *n* rape
våning floor (level, etage in
  building)
våtservetter för barn baby wipes
väderleksrapport weather
  forecast
väg road
vägkarta road map
välkommen welcome
välling baby formula
vän friend
vänster left (direction)
vänta wait
värde *n* value
värdesak *n* valuable
värme heat
väska bag
väster west
växel *n* change (money)
växelkontor currency exchange
  office
växelkursen exchange rate
växla change money

Y

yr dizzy
ytterliggare further (more)

Å

å stream
åka *v* travel, drive (motor vehicle)
åksjuka motion sickness [travel
  sickness BE]
ålder age
återlämna *v* return (give back)
äkta authentic

äkthetsbevis certificate of
  authenticity
älska *v* love
ändra *v* change (reservation)
ändra på *v* alter
änka widow
änkling widower
äta *v* eat

Ö

ögonblick (one) moment
öppet open
öppettider business hours
  [opening hours BE]
öppna *v* open
öra ear
öre öre (Swedish currency)
örhänge earring
öster east
över across (the road)
överfall mugging
övergångsställe för fotgängare
  pedestrian crossing
översätta *v* translate
övervikts bagage excess baggage